CRIMINAL LAW

Second edition

Mark Thomas
Samantha Pegg

Series editors: Amy Sixsmith and David Sixsmith

REVISE
SQE

First published in 2021 by Fink Publishing Ltd
Second edition published in 2023

British Library Cataloguing in Publication Data
A catalogue record for this book is available from the British Library
ISBN: 9781914213687

This book is also available in various ebook formats.
Ebook ISBN: 9781914213694

Multiple-choice questions advisor: Mark Thomas
Cover and text design by BMLD (bmld.uk)
Production and typesetting by Westchester Publishing Services (UK)
Commissioning by R Taylor Publishing Services
Development editing by Peter Hooper
Editorial management by Llinos Edwards
Indexing by Terence Halliday

Fink Publishing Ltd
E-mail: hello@revise4law.co.uk
www.revise4law.co.uk

Contents

This book incorporates the updates to the SQE Assessment Specification published in April 2023 which came into force from 1 September 2023. Please note that, unless otherwise expressly stated, the law covered in this book applies in both England and Wales.

Contributors

THE AUTHORS

Mark Thomas is a practising barrister, and has taught law for several years at both undergraduate and postgraduate levels, including the Legal Practice Course. Mark has published academic textbooks in the field of criminal law and evidence, and has extensive experience in writing revision-style books for law students. He is also the co-author of *Revise SQE: Criminal Law* and editor of *Revise SQE: Ethics and Professional Conduct*, *FLK1 Practice Assessment* and *FLK2 Practice Assessment*. Mark acts as MCQ adviser and reviewer for the Revise SQE series.

Samantha Pegg is a senior lecturer and course leader, specialising in criminal law. She has taught for 20 years at undergraduate and postgraduate (GDL) level and undertakes research in criminal law and legal history. She has published on sexual offences, criminal law and the role of the media in reporting criminality.

SERIES EDITORS

Amy Sixsmith is a senior lecturer in law and programme leader for LLB at the University of Sunderland, and a senior fellow of the Higher Education Academy.

David Sixsmith is assistant professor at Northumbria Law School, and a senior fellow of the Higher Education Academy.

Introduction to Revise SQE

Welcome to *Revise SQE*, a new series of revision guides designed to help you in your preparation for, and achievement in, the Solicitors Qualifying Examination 1 (SQE1) assessment. SQE1 is designed to assess what the Solicitors Regulation Authority (SRA) refer to as 'functioning legal knowledge' (FLK); this is the legal knowledge and competencies required of a newly qualified solicitor in England and Wales. The SRA has chosen single best answer multiple-choice questions (MCQs) to test this knowledge, and *Revise SQE* is here to help.

PREPARING YOURSELF FOR SQE

The SQE is the new route to qualification for aspiring solicitors, introduced in September 2021 as one of the final stages towards qualification as a solicitor. The SQE consists of two parts:

SQE1
- **Functioning legal knowledge (FLK)**
- two x 180 MCQs
- closed book; assessed by two sittings, over 10 hours in total.

SQE2
- **Practical legal skills**
- 16 written and oral assessments
- assesses six practical legal skills, over 14 hours in total.

In addition to the above, any candidate will have to undertake two years' qualifying work experience. More information on the SQE assessments can be found on the SRA website; this revision guide series will focus on FLK and preparation for SQE1.

It is important to note that the SQE can be perceived to be a 'harder' set of assessments than the Legal Practice Course (LPC). The reason for this, explained by the SRA, is that the LPC is designed to prepare candidates for 'day one' of their training contract; the SQE, on the other hand, is designed to prepare candidates for 'day one' of being a newly qualified solicitor. Indeed, the SRA has chosen the SQE1 assessment to be 'closed book' (ie without permitting use of any materials) on the basis that a newly qualified solicitor would know all of the information tested, without having to refer to books or other sources.

With that in mind, and a different style of assessments in place, it is understandable that many readers may feel nervous or wary of the SQE. This is especially so given that this style of assessment is likely to be different from what readers will have experienced before. In this *Introduction* and revision guide series, we hope to alleviate some of those concerns with guidance on preparing for the SQE assessment, tips on how to approach single best answer MCQs and expertly written guides to aid in your revision.

What does SQE1 entail?

SQE1 consists of two assessments, containing 180 single best answer MCQs each (360 MCQs in total). The table below breaks down what is featured in each of these assessments.

Assessment	Contents of assessment ('functioning legal knowledge')
FLK assessment 1	• Business law and practice • Dispute resolution • Contract • Tort • The legal system (the legal system of England and Wales and sources of law, constitutional and administrative law and European Union law and legal services)
FLK assessment 2	• Property practice • Wills and the administration of estates • Solicitors accounts • Land law • Trusts • Criminal law and practice

Please be aware that in addition to the above, ethics and professional conduct will be examined pervasively across the two assessments (ie it could crop up anywhere).

Each substantive topic is allocated a percentage of the assessment paper (eg 'legal services' will form 12–16% of the FLK1 assessment) and is broken down further into 'core principles'. Candidates are advised to read the SQE1 Assessment Specification in full (available on the SRA website). We have also provided a *Revise SQE checklist* to help you in your preparation and revision for SQE1 (see below).

HOW DO I PREPARE FOR SQE1?

Given the vastly different nature of SQE1 compared to anything you may have done previously, it can be quite daunting to consider how you could possibly prepare for 360 single best answer MCQs, spanning 11 different substantive topics (especially given that it is 'closed book'). The *Revise SQE FAQ* below, however, will set you off on the right path to success.

Revise SQE FAQ

Question	Answer
1. Where do I start?	We would advise that you begin by reviewing the assessment specification for SQE1. You need to identify what subject matter can be assessed under each substantive topic. For each topic, you should honestly ask yourself whether you would be prepared to answer an MCQ on that topic in SQE1.
	We have helped you in this process by providing a *Revise SQE checklist* on our website (revise4law. co.uk) that allows you to read the subject matter of each topic and identify where you consider your knowledge to be at any given time. We have also helpfully cross-referenced each topic to a chapter and page of our *Revise SQE* revision guides.
2. Do I need to know legal authorities, such as case law?	In the majority of circumstances, candidates are not required to know or use legal authorities. This includes statutory provisions, case law or procedural rules. Of course, candidates will need to be aware of legal principles deriving from common law and statute.
	There may be occasions, however, where the assessment specification does identify a legal authority (such as *Rylands v Fletcher* in tort law). In this case, candidates will be required to know the name of that case, the principles of that case and how to apply that case to the facts of an MCQ. These circumstances are clearly highlighted in the assessment specification and candidates are advised to ensure they engage with those legal authorities in full.

Revise SQE FAQ (Continued)

Question	Answer
3. Do I need to know the history behind a certain area of law?	While understanding the history and development of a certain area of law is beneficial, there is no requirement for you to know or prepare for any questions relating to the development of the law (eg in criminal law, candidates will not need to be aware of the development from objective to subjective recklessness). SQE1 will be testing a candidate's knowledge of the law as it stands four calendar months prior to the date of the first assessment in an assessment window.
4. Do I need to be aware of academic opinion or proposed reforms to the law?	Candidates preparing for SQE1 do not need to focus on critical evaluation of the law, or proposed reforms to the law either.
5. How do I prepare for single best answer MCQs?	See our separate *Revise SQE* guide on preparing for single best answer MCQs below.

Where does *Revise SQE* come into it?

The *Revise SQE* series of revision guides is designed to aid your revision and consolidate your understanding; the series is not designed to replace your substantive learning of the SQE1 topics. We hope that this series will provide clarity as to assessment focus, useful tips for sitting SQE1 and act as a general revision aid.

There are also materials on our website to help you prepare and revise for the SQE1, such as a *Revise SQE checklist*. This *checklist* is designed to help you identify which substantive topics you feel confident about heading into the exam – see below for an example.

Revise SQE checklist

Criminal law

SQE content	Corresponding chapter	Revise SQE checklist		
Criminal damage • Simple criminal damage	Chapter 9, pages 208–218	I do not know this subject and I am not ready for SQE1 ☐	I partially know this subject, but I am not ready for SQE1 ☐	I know this subject and I am ready for SQE1 ☐

Criminal law (Continued)

SQE content	Corresponding chapter	Revise SQE checklist		
Criminal damage • Aggravated criminal damage	Chapter 9, pages 218–221	I do not know this subject and I am not ready for SQE1 ☐	I partially know this subject, but I am not ready for SQE1 ☐	I know this subject and I am ready for SQE1 ☐
Criminal damage • Arson	Chapter 9, pages 221–223	I do not know this subject and I am not ready for SQE1 ☐	I partially know this subject, but I am not ready for SQE1 ☐	I know this subject and I am ready for SQE1 ☐

PREPARING FOR SINGLE BEST ANSWER MCQS

As discussed above, SQE1 will be a challenging assessment for all candidates. This is partly due to the quantity of information a candidate must be aware of in two separate sittings. In addition, however, an extra complexity is added due to the nature of the assessment itself: MCQs.

The SRA has identified that MCQs are the most appropriate way to test a candidate's knowledge and understanding of fundamental legal principles. While this may be the case, it is likely that many candidates have little, if any, experience of MCQs as part of their previous study. Even if a candidate does have experience of MCQs, SQE1 will feature a special form of MCQs known as 'single best answer' questions.

What are single best answer MCQs and what do they look like?

Single best answer MCQs are a specialised form of question, used extensively in other fields such as in training medical professionals. The idea behind single best answer MCQs is that the multitude of options available to a candidate may each bear merit, sharing commonalities and correct statements of law or principle, but only one option is absolutely correct (in the sense that it is the 'best' answer). In this regard, single best answer MCQs are different from traditional MCQs. A traditional MCQ will feature answers that are implausible in the sense that the distractors are 'obviously wrong'. Indeed, distractors in a traditional MCQ are often very dissimilar, resulting in a candidate being able to spot answers that are clearly wrong with greater ease.

In a well-constructed single best answer MCQ, on the other hand, each option should look equally attractive given their similarities and subtle differences. The skill of the candidate will be identifying which, out of the options provided, is the single best answer. This requires a much greater level of engagement with the question than a traditional MCQ would require; candidates must take the time to read the questions carefully in the exam.

For SQE1, single best answer MCQs will be structured as follows:

A woman is charged with battery, having thrown a rock towards another person intending to scare them. The rock hits the person in the head, causing no injury. The woman claims that she never intended that the rock hit the person, but the prosecution allege that the woman was reckless as to whether the rock would hit the other person.

The factual scenario. First, the candidate will be provided with a factual scenario that sets the scene for the question to be asked.

Which of the following is the most accurate statement regarding the test for recklessness in relation to a battery?

The question. Next, the candidate will be provided with the question (known as the 'stem') that they must find the single best answer to.

A. There must have been a risk that force would be applied by the rock, and that the reasonable person would have foreseen that risk and unjustifiably taken it.

B. There must have been a risk that force would be applied by the rock, and that the woman should have foreseen that risk and unjustifiably taken it.

The possible answers. Finally, the candidate will be provided with **five** possible answers. There is only one single best answer that must be chosen. The other answers, known as 'distractors', are not the 'best' answer available.

C. There must have been a risk that force would be applied by the rock, and that the woman must have foreseen that risk and unjustifiably taken it.

D. There must have been a risk that force would be applied by the rock, and that both the woman and the reasonable person should have foreseen that risk and unjustifiably taken it.

E. There must have been a risk that force would be applied by the rock, but there is no requirement that the risk be foreseen.

Now that you know what the MCQs will look like on SQE1, let us talk about how you may go about tackling an MCQ.

How do I tackle single best answer MCQs?

No exact art exists in terms of answering single best answer MCQs; your success depends on your subject knowledge and understanding of how that subject knowledge can be applied. Despite this, there are tips and tricks that may be helpful for you to consider when confronted with a single best answer MCQ.

1. Read the question twice	2. Understand the question being asked	3. If you know the answer outright	4. If not, employ a process of elimination	5. Take an educated and reasoned guess	6. Skip and come back to it later

1. Read the entire question at least twice

This sounds obvious but is so often overlooked. You are advised to read the entire question once, taking in all relevant pieces of information, understanding what the question is asking you and being aware of the options available. Once you have done that, read the entire question again and this time pay careful attention to the wording that is used.

- **In the factual scenario:** Does it use any words that stand out? Do any words used have legal bearing? What are you told and what are you not told?
- **In the stem:** What are you being asked? Are there certain words to look out for (eg 'should', 'must', 'will', 'shall')?
- **In the answers:** What are the differences between each option? Are they substantial differences or subtle differences? Do any differences turn on a word or a phrase?

You should be prepared to give each question at least two viewings to mitigate any misunderstandings or oversights.

2. Understand the question being asked

It is important first that you understand what the question is asking of you. The SRA has identified that the FLK assessments may consist of single best answer MCQs that, for example,

- require the candidate to simply identify a correct legal principle or rule
- require the candidate to not only identify the correct legal principle or rule, but also apply that principle or rule to the factual scenario
- provide the candidate with the correct legal principle or rule, but require the candidate to identify how it should be properly applied and/or the outcome of that proper application.

By first identifying what the question is seeking you to do, you can then understand what the creators of that question are seeking to test and how to approach the answers available.

3. If you know the answer outright

You may feel as though a particular answer 'jumps out' at you, and that you are certain it is correct. It is very likely that the answer is correct. While you should be confident in your answers, do not allow your confidence (and perhaps overconfidence) to rush you into making a decision. Review all of your options one final time before you move on to the next question.

4. If you do not know the answer outright, employ a process of elimination

There may be situations in which the answer is not obvious from the outset. This may be due to the close similarities between different answers. Remember, it is the 'single best answer' that you are looking for. If you keep this in your mind, it will thereafter be easier to employ a process of elimination. Identify which answers you are sure are not correct (or not the 'best') and whittle down your options. Once you have only two options remaining, carefully scrutinise the wording used in both answers and look back to the question being asked. Identify what you consider to the be the best answer, in light of that question. Review your answer and move on to the next question.

5. Take an educated and reasoned guess

There may be circumstances, quite commonly, in which you do not know the answer to the question. In this circumstance, you should try as hard as possible to eliminate any distractors that you are positive are incorrect and then take an educated and reasoned guess based on the options available.

6. Skip and come back to it later

If time permits, you may think it appropriate to skip a question that you are unsure of and return to it before the end of the assessment. If you do so, we would advise

- that you make a note of what question you have skipped (for ease of navigation later on), and
- ensure you leave sufficient time for you to go back to that question before the end of the assessment.

The same advice is applicable to any question that you have answered but for which you remain unsure.

We hope that this brief guide will assist you in your preparation towards, and engagement with, single best answer MCQs.

GUIDED TOUR

Each chapter contains a number of features to help you revise, apply and test your knowledge.

Make sure you know   Each chapter begins with an overview of the main topics covered and why you need to understand them for the purpose of the SQE1 assessments.

SQE assessment advice   This identifies what you need to pay particular attention to in your revision as you work through the chapter.

What do you know already?   These questions help you to assess which topics you feel confident with and which topics you may need to spend more time on (and where to find them in the chapter).

Key term   Key terms are highlighted in bold where they first appear and defined in a separate box.

Exam warning   This feature offers advice on where it is possible to go wrong in the assessments.

Revision tip   Throughout the chapters are ideas to help you revise effectively and be best prepared for the assessment.

Summary   This handy box brings together key information in an easy to revise and remember form.

Practice example   These examples take a similar format to SQE-type questions and provide an opportunity to see how content might be applied to a scenario.

Procedural link   Where relevant, this element shows how a concept might apply to another procedural topic in the series.

Key point checklist   At the end of each chapter there is a bullet-point summary of its most important content.

Key terms and concepts   These are listed at the end of each chapter to help ensure you know, or can revise, terms and concepts you will need to be familiar with for the assessments.

SQE-style questions Five SQE-style questions on the chapter topic give you an opportunity to test your knowledge.

Answers to questions Check how you did with answers to both the quick knowledge test from the start of the chapter and the SQE questions at the end of the chapter.

Key cases, rules, statutes and instruments These list the key sources candidates need to be familiar with for the SQE assessment.

SQE1 TABLE OF LEGAL AUTHORITIES

The SQE1 Assessment Specification states the following in respect of legal authorities and their relevance to SQE1:

> On occasion in legal practice a case name or statutory provision, for example, is the term normally used to describe a legal principle or an area of law, or a rule or procedural step (eg *Rylands v Fletcher*, CPR Part 36, Section 25 notice). In such circumstances, candidates are required to know and be able to use such case names, statutory provisions etc. In all other circumstances candidates are not required to recall specific case names, or cite statutory or regulatory authorities.

This *SQE1 table of legal authorities* identifies the legal authorities you are required to know for the purpose of the SQE1 Functioning Legal Knowledge assessments for *Criminal Law*.

Legal authority	Corresponding *Revise SQE* chapter/pages
Offences Against the Person Act 1861	**Chapter 6: Non-fatal offences against the person**
s 47	134–137
s 20	137–141
s 18	141–143
Theft Act 1968	**Chapter 7: Theft offences**
s 1	151–163
s 8	163–167
s 9	167–172
s 10	172–175

TABLE OF CASES

TABLE OF STATUTES

The SQE1 Assessment Specification requires you to know the statutes in bold below.

General principles of criminal law

■ MAKE SURE YOU KNOW

This chapter will cover the core principles of criminal liability. You are required to understand the terms actus reus and mens rea, and the legal principles that flow from those terms. You are required to be able to apply these legal principles and rules appropriately and effectively to realistic client-based and ethical problems and situations for your SQE1 assessment.

The SQE1 Assessment Specification has not identified that candidates are required to recall/recite any case names, or statutory materials, for actus reus and mens rea.

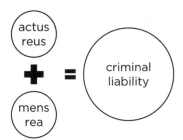

Overview of criminal liability

■ SQE ASSESSMENT ADVICE

As you work through this chapter, remember to pay particular attention in your revision to:
• the elements of a criminal offence
• the meaning of actus reus
• omissions liability
• establishing causation
• the various mens rea terms
• the requirement of contemporaneity.

■ WHAT DO YOU KNOW ALREADY?

Have a go at these questions before reading this chapter. If you find some difficult or cannot remember the answers, make a note to look more closely at that area during your revision.

1) Fill in the blank: the actus reus of an offence generally refers to

   _____.

   [Actus reus, pages 3–12]
2) Can you be criminally liable for an omission to act?

   [Omissions liability, pages 4–7]
3) True or false: an interference by a third party will always break the chain of causation and relieve the defendant of liability.

   [Legal causation, pages 8–12]
4) What direction must be given to the jury when they are deciding whether a defendant has oblique (indirect) intent?

   [Oblique intention, pages 12–13]

INTRODUCTION TO GENERAL PRINCIPLES OF CRIMINAL LAW

To begin with, we are concerned with the fundamental elements of a criminal offence. These are labelled the **actus reus** and **mens rea**.

Key term: actus reus

Actus reus broadly translates as 'guilty act' and refers to all elements of an offence that are not concerned with the state of mind of the defendant (D). It is worth noting that the actus reus of an offence does not have to be a positive act. For example, murder requires a 'killing' and this may be by way of a positive act or an omission.

Key term: mens rea

Mens rea is the term used to represent the state of mind required of D (also known as the fault element). Mens rea is either subjective (concerned with D's state of mind) or objective (assessed by reference to the reasonable person).

Most of the offences within this revision guide require that a particular result is brought about. These are called *result crimes*. For these offences you must also consider the principles of **causation**.

Key term: causation

Causation is concerned with culpability, or responsibility, and requires you to identify whether D should be held criminally culpable for a result that has been brought about.

Those offences that do not require a result to be brought about are called *conduct crimes*. We identify what crimes are 'conduct' and 'result' throughout the remaining chapters.

ACTUS REUS

The actus reus of an offence is set out in the relevant statutory or common-law definition. The actus reus provides the elements of the offence that must be established by the prosecution to prove the defendant's guilt. These may include an act or an omission, but may also require that particular circumstances exist, or that a specific result is brought about.

For example, the actus reus of murder is the 'unlawful killing of a human being within the King's peace'. This definition gives us the elements that must be established for criminal liability. There is no defined act or omission that must be proven, but the offence requires three circumstances are proven: that the victim is a human, that the killing takes place during peace time, and the killing is unlawful. It also requires one result: the death of the victim (see **Chapter 5**).

Let us consider some general actus reus principles that could be relevant to the SQE1 assessment.

The actus reus must be voluntary

The defendant must have consciously committed the actus reus of the alleged offence or he cannot be criminally liable. By conscious commission, we mean that he must have been doing something voluntarily, under his own volition. If his muscles are not being controlled by his conscious mind, he cannot be said to be acting voluntarily. For example:

- Sam strikes out to swat a wasp in her car and loses control of the car, hitting a pedestrian.
- Mark falls down the stairs and, while plummeting, strikes Sam with his foot.
- Sam sneezes and reflexively throws the dinner plate she is drying. The plate hits Mark on the nose.

However, the defendant cannot escape liability simply because they cannot control an impulse to act, or if they argue that they did not intend to bring about that result – their conduct must be truly involuntary.

In many cases, this will be as a result of what is termed 'automatism'. This is a specific defence that requires a total loss of control that stems from an external cause. **Chapter 4** explores where that external cause is a non-dangerous drug, but automatism may also result from something as simple as concussion.

Exam warning

Be aware that the SQE1 Assessment Specification does not expressly require you to know the substantive defence of automatism.
Automatism is, however, a fundamental aspect of criminal liability generally, in that it must be proven that D acted voluntarily. Keep an eye out for those circumstances where D's conduct may not be voluntary.

Omissions liability

An omission is a failure to act. As our system of law focuses upon prohibiting certain acts, the general position is that individuals are not liable for offences based upon their failure to act. However, this is subject to some significant caveats. **Figure 1.1** identifies the process to undertake when considering omissions liability.

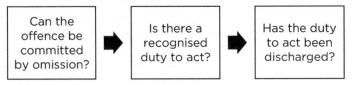

| Can the offence be committed by omission? | ➡ | Is there a recognised duty to act? | ➡ | Has the duty to act been discharged? |

Figure 1.1: Omissions liability

Can the offence be committed by omission?

First, you need to identify whether the offence in question is capable of being committed by omission. For each offence considered in this revision guide, we will identify whether it can be committed by omission. By way of example, while murder may be committed by omission, unlawful act manslaughter cannot (see **Chapter 5**).

Is there a recognised duty to act?

The next issue is whether you are in a position that imposes a legal duty to act (rather than a moral duty). The common law has established a number of exceptions to the general principle that you are not liable for a failure to act. These are detailed in **Table 1.1**.

Practice example 1.1

Carly is a heroin addict who has moved in with her mother. Her half-sister Gemma visits their mother's house, bringing Carly some heroin that Carly then self-injects. It rapidly becomes obvious that Carly has overdosed and, although Gemma and her mother take steps to make Carly comfortable, they do not call for an ambulance as they are concerned they may get into trouble. Carly dies as a result of an overdose. Gemma is charged with gross negligence manslaughter, but Gemma must be under a duty to act to be liable.

Does Gemma owe a duty to Carly and, if so, under which category is a duty imposed?

These were the facts of *R v Evans* [2009] EWCA Crim 650. Here the court discussed the possibility of a duty arising under relationship (as Carly was Gemma's half-sister), through an assumption of care (as she took steps to look after her) and creation of/contribution to a dangerous situation. A duty does not have to be established by using only one exceptional category.

Table 1.1: Recognised duty categories

Duty category	Explanation
Statutory or contractual duty	A duty may be imposed by statute.
	Where a failure to fulfil a contractual term poses a risk of death, a duty to act is imposed. For example, in *R v Pittwood* (1902) 19 TLR 37, a railway employee neglected to close the gate to prevent the railway line being crossed when a train was coming. A road user was hit by the train and killed when crossing the tracks.
	In *R v Dytham* [1979] QB 722, a police officer saw a man being beaten and did not intervene. The man died as a result. The officer was under a duty to act by virtue of his position. This duty flowed from his contractual obligation, or his position of public office.
Special relationship	A duty may arise from a close relationship, though it is likely this only extends to parents (or guardians) and their young children.
	In *R v Gibbins and Proctor* (1919) 13 Cr App R 134, a father and his partner intentionally starved the man's child to death. The father was convicted of murder as he was under a duty as the child's father. His partner was also liable as she had assumed responsibility for the child (see below).
Voluntary assumption of responsibility	Where an individual takes steps to assume responsibility for another who is unable to care for themselves due to, for example, age or illness, a duty is imposed.
	In *R v Stone and Dobinson* [1977] QB 354, Stone's sister (Fanny) came to live with Stone and his partner. Both Stone and Dobinson were mentally impaired, and Fanny suffered from anorexia. The couple initially cared for Fanny but as her condition deteriorated the couple were unable to cope, stopped attempting to care for her and Fanny died. The couple were convicted of gross negligence manslaughter.

Table 1.1: Continued

Duty category	Explanation
Creation of/contribution to a dangerous situation	Where D inadvertently creates a dangerous situation, he is under a duty to act to rectify that situation.
	In *R v Miller* [1983] 2 AC 161, a squatter fell asleep and set fire to a mattress he was sleeping on with his cigarette. Upon waking he made no attempt to extinguish the fire or call the fire service, instead he moved to another room. He was convicted of arson (see **Chapter 9**). It was held that as he had created a danger and was aware he had done so, a duty to act would be imposed.
	The courts have since moved away from this purely subjective approach and a duty may now also be imposed where a person merely *contributes* to a situation that they know or *ought to know* has become life threatening (refer back to **Practice example 1.1**).

Has the duty to act been discharged?

Lastly, in order to be liable, the defendant must fail to discharge their duty to act. To discharge a duty, you must merely take reasonable steps. What amounts to reasonable steps will depend upon the situation and you need to look out for this in SQE1. For example, a lifeguard – contractually obliged to monitor safety at a swimming pool – would be expected upon spotting a drowning swimmer to attempt a rescue. Leaving poolside to fetch a fellow lifeguard (as he did not want to get his hair wet that day) would be unreasonable and would not discharge that duty.

Causation

Where an offence requires that a particular result is brought about, the prosecution must also prove that the defendant *caused* that result.

In short, what you are looking for in an SQE scenario is an unbroken set of events that has led to the result. If the defendant cannot be said to be responsible because he had not contributed to that result, or his contribution was diminished to insignificance as another party had played a greater role in bringing about the result, then he cannot be held criminally culpable.

In most cases, causation will be a straightforward question. In more difficult cases, consider the process in **Figure 1.2**.

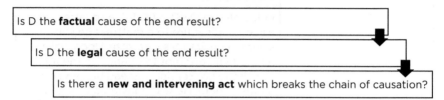

Figure 1.2: Elements of causation

Factual causation

First, the defendant must be the factual cause of the result. This is established through the 'but for' test; 'but for the defendant's actions, would the prohibited result have occurred?' If the result would have happened regardless, then the defendant is not responsible.

When the defendant is charged with a homicide offence, this means we must find that there has been an *acceleration* of death – as everyone will (eventually) die (see **Practice example 1.2**).

Practice example 1.2

John puts potassium cyanide (a poison) into his mother's drink, intending to kill her. She dies that night, but it is established that she had died of natural causes before the poison took effect.

Has John, in fact, caused her death?

These were the facts of *R v White* [1910] 2 KB 124. John could not be the factual cause of death as his mother would have died when she did regardless of his act. John was liable, however, for attempted murder (see Chapter 3).

If factual causation is satisfied, the next step is to establish legal causation.

Legal causation

The second test is whether the defendant is *legally* culpable. There are a number of key principles you need to be aware of. These are outlined in **Table 1.2**.

Table 1.2: Understanding legal causation

Principle	Explanation and examples
D need only be a more than minimal cause of the prohibited result	D must be the 'substantial' cause of the result, though this has been held to mean 'more than slight and trifling'.
	For example, in *R v Pagett* (1983) 76 Cr App R 279, D shot at the police officers who were attempting to arrest him. The officers returned fire and killed a young girl who D was using as a human shield. D was convicted of manslaughter as he was a substantial cause of the result and the officers had not broken the chain of causation.
D need not be the only cause of the result	There may be several causes that bring about the result, and D need not be the only cause as long as he is a 'substantial' cause.
	In *R v Benge* (1865) 4 F & F 504, D, a railway foreman misread a train timetable when a section of the track was being raised. Flagmen were supposed to wave a warning if a train was approaching but were not at the correct distance. The train hit the raised track, resulting in several deaths. Despite the fact that a number of acts (including that of the train driver who was not paying full attention) contributed to the deaths, D could still be held responsible.
D must be the operating cause	D must be the operating cause at the time of death (ie there is no break in the chain of causation).
	In *R v Smith* [1959] 2 QB 35, D had stabbed a comrade during a fight. V was carried to the hospital and dropped twice in the process. When he arrived at the hospital he was not examined fully and left to bleed to death. A blood transfusion would have saved his life. D was still responsible for V's death as the stab wound he had delivered was still the 'operating and substantial' cause of death.

Exam warning

Make sure that you do not confuse the causation principles in criminal law with those studied in tort law. While factual causation is the same in both areas of law, legal causation is an additional hurdle in criminal law cases.

New and intervening acts

As outlined in **Table 1.2**, the defendant must be the operating cause of the prohibited result. The defendant will not be liable for that offence if there is a break in the chain of causation – if an intervening event means that he can no longer be said to be the true cause of the result. The SQE1 assessment may require you to know any of the following intervening acts:

- Acts by the victim:
  - The victim will break the chain of causation if he acts in a way that is informed and voluntary (ie self-injecting drugs he has been supplied with, and so bringing about his own death).
  - Where the victim causes or contributes to his own injuries or his own demise this may be attributable to the defendant if the victim's actions were 'proportionate' to the threat posed (see *R v Roberts* (1972) 56 Cr App R 95 in **Chapter 6**). For example, Mark runs into the path of a car and suffers serious injuries while trying to escape from Sam, who was threatening him with a knife. This is a proportionate response and Sam will be responsible for the serious injuries inflicted. Only where the response is unreasonable (or 'daft') will it break the chain.
  - Where the victim neglects injuries inflicted by the defendant (ie by failing to seek treatment after being stabbed), the defendant will remain responsible for the extent of the injuries suffered (see **Take your victim as you find them**).
- A 'free, deliberate and informed' intervention by a third party:
  - An independent third party may intervene and break the chain of causation if their action is 'free, independent and informed'. For example, if Mark punches Sam and, while she is laying on the floor, Jensen (who has a grudge against Sam) runs over and stabs her to death, Mark will not be responsible for her death (merely the original injuries). In *Pagett*, considered in **Table 1.2**, the chain of causation was not broken by the police officers as they were not acting 'freely' when they were forced to return fire.
- Medical treatment:
  - Our starting point is that it is highly unusual for medical treatment (or medical neglect) to break the chain of causation. Treatment that is merely negligent will not break the chain of causation.
  - To break the chain, the treatment must be an independent act that is 'so potent' that the defendant's contribution is insignificant. The treatment (or lack thereof) must be 'so overwhelming' that it makes the original injury 'part of the history'. This potent and independent act must amount to treatment that can be characterised as 'palpably wrong'.

- Unforeseeable natural causes:
  - 'Acts of God' will only break the chain when they are both unforeseeable to the reasonable person and were unforeseen by the defendant. For example, suppose Mark leaves Sam injured and unable to move on a beach at low tide. Mark will be responsible for Sam's death when Sam drowns as it is foreseeable that the tide will come in. But where Mark leaves Sam injured and unable to move in her garden, and Sam dies as a result of being struck by lightning, Mark will not be responsible for her death.

Exam warning

Try to remember that the chain of causation can be broken in three main ways: by acts of a third party, by acts of the victim and by acts of God (ie a natural unforeseeable event). If you are faced with a multiple-choice question (MCQ) assessing causation, keep an eye out for one of these three intervening acts.

Take your victim as you find them

A factor that cannot break the chain of causation is an inherent weakness of the victim. Suppose Sam punches Mark, who has an abnormally thin skull. She will be responsible for Mark's death despite the fact Mark is abnormally sensitive to injury.

This principle extends further than physical vulnerabilities. Consider the following examples:
- A man cut the victim's finger. The victim refused medical treatment and died of tetanus (a bacterial infection).
- A woman who was a Jehovah's Witness refused a blood transfusion after being stabbed as her religion did not allow her to undergo that procedure. She died from her injuries.

In both of these cases, the defendants were held responsible for the deaths of their victims. In the first, the judge merely directed the jury to ask whether the injury was the actual cause of death. In the modern day, failing to seek treatment for a relatively minor injury may seem unreasonable, but in the second example, the court made it clear that it is irrelevant whether the victim's response is reasonable.

Summary: what do we know about actus reus?

What is actus reus concerned with?	Actus reus refers to the external elements of a crime and is concerned with the conduct, circumstances and results (if any) of a crime.

Does the actus reus require an 'act'?	While most crimes will be committed by way of a positive act, it is possible for many offences to be committed by a failure to act (ie an omission). In order for this to be the case, the crime has to be capable of being committed by omission and there must be a legal duty on D to act.
What is the test for causation in criminal law?	The magistrates or jury must be satisfied that D was the factual (ie 'but for') cause of harm, as well as being the legal cause of harm. As part of causation, there must not be a new and intervening act that breaks the chain of causation.

MENS REA

The following discusses the common mens rea terms of intention, subjective recklessness and negligence.

Intention

Intention is the highest standard of mens rea required for serious offences such as murder (see **Chapter 5**) and causing grievous bodily harm with intent (see **Chapter 6**).

Intention has been given two different interpretations in criminal law: **direct intention** and **oblique intention**. Both are subjective, focusing on the defendant's state of mind at the time the actus reus is performed.

Key term: direct intention

Direct intention is where it is D's aim or purpose to bring about a prohibited result. For example, Sam points a gun at Mark, intending to kill him, and pulls the trigger.

Key term: oblique intention

Oblique intention is where it is not D's aim or purpose to bring about a prohibited result, but he foresees that result as virtually certain to occur as a result of his actions. For example, Mark intends to kill Sam by shooting her and Sam is standing behind a window. His direct intent will be to kill Sam, but his oblique intent will be to break the glass.

There is no statutory definition of intention, and its meaning has been established in common law.

Direct intention

Motive and desire are irrelevant to the question of whether someone has direct intent. We can establish whether it is your aim or purpose to bring about a consequence without asking why you have acted in that way. For example, you can desperately wish that someone does not have to die, yet still intend to kill them.

Oblique intention

Oblique intention is not a different type of intention, it is merely a way of finding intention. A direction on oblique intention will only be given in cases where it is not the defendant's aim or purpose to bring about the prohibited result. Consider the following examples:

• Sam sets fire to a house as she has a grudge against the resident. Her purpose is not to kill any of the residents, but a child dies in the fire.
• Mark throws his infant child towards his pram as he has lost his temper. He intended for the child to land in his pram, but the child hits the floor and dies.

The key test for oblique intent is that laid out by Lord Steyn in *Woollin* [1999] 1 AC 82 and is detailed in **Figure 1.3**.

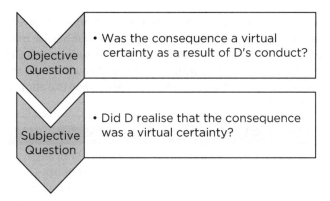

Figure 1.3: Test for oblique intention

Revision tip

Only foresight by D of a *virtual certainty* will suffice. Where the result is seen as a possible, probable, or even highly probable consequence, D may be reckless (see **Subjective recklessness**), but he *does not* intend to bring about that consequence. Pay close attention to the wording of an MCQ to identify whether the result was actually a virtual certainty or not.

Exam warning

Despite the fact there is an objective element, virtual certainty is, overall, a subjective test. The jury must conclude that D foresaw the prohibited consequence as a virtually certain result of his actions. Do not allow an MCQ to trick you into thinking that D is not required to foresee the result as being virtually certain (see **Practice example 1.3**).

Practice example 1.3

Barbara has planted a bomb in her local supermarket as they had recently fired her son from his Saturday job. Her aim is to cause the supermarket to lose revenue by forcing its closure. She calls in a warning an hour before the bomb is timed to explode, but the bomb explodes early, killing a police officer. Barbara is charged with murder and the judge directs the jury that as it was virtually certain the bomb would cause death or serious injury, they are bound to find that Barbara had the necessary intention.

Has the judge correctly directed the jury?

The direction that must be given is that from *Woollin* (above) and the judge has not given the jury that direction, nor has he made clear that it is a decision for them to reach on the facts. As Barbara called in a timely warning, it would be difficult to conclude that she had the necessary intention as she anticipated that the shop would be empty when the bomb exploded.

Exam warning

Importantly, foresight of a virtually certain result is *not* equivalent to intention; such foresight is only *evidence* of an intention. This means that the jury are not bound to find that D intended a result that was virtually certain. An MCQ may suggest that foresight of a virtually certain result means that the jury *must* find that D intended that result. Do not allow yourself to be confused by this.

Subjective recklessness

Recklessness is concerned with unjustifiable risk-taking and is satisfied where the jury can be sure of two things (see **Figure 1.4**).

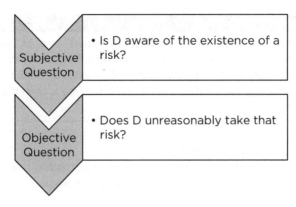

Figure 1.4: Subjective recklessness

Awareness of a risk

To amount to subjective recklessness, the risk must be seen by the defendant; if he does not foresee the risk, he cannot be reckless. This is the case even where that risk would have been evident to the reasonable prudent person.

The defendant's characteristics are taken into account in assessing whether he had appreciated the risk. This will include his age, mental state, the situation in which he finds himself and any other relevant factors (see **Practice example 1.4**).

Practice example 1.4

A man suffering from schizophrenia is looking for somewhere warm to sleep and settles in a haystack. As it is cold, he lights a fire in the haystack. The fire spreads and causes substantial damage. He is charged with arson (see **Chapter 9**). The trial judge directed the jury that they could convict him of this offence (which requires D to have intentionally or recklessly destroyed or damaged property), even if he had not recognised there was a risk of damage or had closed his mind to that risk.

Has the judge correctly directed the jury?

These are the facts of _R v Stephenson_ [1979] QB 695. The Court of Appeal quashed the conviction as the test should have been given as a purely subjective one. D's schizophrenia may have prevented him from recognising the risk and, to be reckless, D _must_ appreciate the risk.

Exam warning

An MCQ may speak about the fact that D 'should have' or 'ought to have' known of the existence of a risk. This is an incorrect statement of law; you should be focusing your attention on words that import a subjective test (eg where D 'knew' or 'knows'). Pay close attention to wording like this.

Unjustifiable taking of the risk

The risk the defendant is taking must be an unjustifiable risk. It must be unreasonable to run the risk of the harmful consequence.

Whether a risk is unjustifiable is an objective question. Many everyday activities we engage in involve a risk of damaging persons or property (eg driving a car, hitting a hard cricket ball in a garden or walking a dog). Whether a risk is unjustifiable is a question for the court and they will take into account the social utility of the activity. For example, overtaking someone at speed on a road may be unjustifiable if you are rushing to meet a friend, but may be justifiable if you are driving your spouse to hospital as they have been injured.

Negligence

Negligence is a failure by the defendant to act in conformity with an objective standard. Unlike intention and recklessness, the focus is not upon the defendant's actual state of mind at the time the actus reus is satisfied. The factfinders will instead be directed to consider how a reasonable person would have acted in those circumstances and whether the defendant's behaviour falls short of that objective standard.

Revision tip

For the purposes of SQE1, negligence is relevant only to the offence of gross negligence manslaughter and is discussed in **Chapter 5.**

Summary: what do we know about mens rea?

What is intention?	Intention can either be direct or oblique. Direct intention is where it is your aim or purpose to bring about the prohibited consequence. Oblique intention is where the result is a virtually certain one and D foresees that result as virtually certain.

What is recklessness?	Recklessness is seeing a risk and going on to take it. It must be an unjustifiable risk and the focus is on whether D saw that risk. As a subjective test, D's characteristics must be taken into account in deciding whether they saw that risk.
What is negligence?	Here we are concerned with the conduct of the accused and whether it fails to meet the standards of the reasonable person.

COINCIDENCE OF ACTUS REUS AND MENS REA

For the defendant to be liable, the prosecution must establish that the relevant actus reus and mens rea elements of the offence coincide. For example, Mark hates Sam and wishes she was dead. He has devised a plan to kill her but, before he gets a chance to execute his plan, he accidentally runs Sam over with his car. Sam had stepped out in front of the car and Mark had not seen her. Mark may have intended to kill, but that mens rea element did not coincide with the prohibited consequence. Therefore, there can be no liability for homicide. Mark's guilty thoughts will not make him liable in this situation due to the lack of contemporaneity.

There are situations where it is in the interests of justice to find that the defendant has the actus reus and mens rea for the offence alleged even though these elements do not exist at precisely the same moment. These are set out in **Table 1.3** (overleaf).

TRANSFERRED MALICE

Where the defendant fulfils the actus reus of an offence, for example, Mark intends to kill Sam by shooting her, but Mark misses and shoots Adam, we can still find liability for murder through the doctrine of **transferred malice**. Here the mens rea (an intention to kill) is transferred from Sam to create liability for the killing of Adam.

Key term: transferred malice

Transferred malice is a legal doctrine that allows for a transfer of mens rea when an offence targeted at a particular individual or piece of property results in injury/damage to a different person or piece of property.

Table 1.3: Contemporaneity in criminal law

Principle	Explanation and examples
Continuing act	Where the actus reus can be satisfied by a continuing act it is sufficient that D has the mens rea at some point while that act is continuing.
	For example, in *Fagan v Metropolitan Police Commissioner* [1969] 1 QB 439, D drove on to a police officer's foot accidently. When the officer told him to move the car, he refused. It was held that he was liable for a battery (see **Chapter 6**). Although D did not initially have mens rea when he applied force, he did when he failed to move the car.
A series of acts	An offence may be committed through a series of acts and D may not have the prescribed mens rea when committing each act. Where this is the case, it is sufficient that D has the mens rea at some point during that series of acts.
	For example, in *Thabo Meli v R* [1954] 1 All ER 373, V was struck numerous times by several men who intended to kill him. When they thought he was dead, his body was rolled over a cliff edge to make his death appear accidental. In fact, he was not dead and later died from exposure. The men had the mens rea for murder at the time of the beating, but the actus reus was not complete (the killing). When they rolled his body off the cliff this had resulted in his death, but they did not intend to kill as they thought he was already dead.
	Please note this must be a series of acts/events – not a series of unconnected events.

There are two limitations to the doctrine of transferred malice:
- The defendant's mens rea can only be transferred when it is for the same offence. If Mark had shot at Sam and missed, but his bullet had broken a window, the mens rea could not be transferred to criminal damage.
- There can be no double or general transfer of mens rea. Where a man stabs a woman intending to kill her, but also injures a foetus she is

carrying, who is later born alive but then dies from their injuries, the mens rea for murder cannot be transferred.

STRICT LIABILITY

There are some offences for which the prosecution is not required to prove mens rea for one or more elements of the actus reus. These include driving offences such as speeding and driving without insurance. Where no mens rea is required *at all*, the offence is termed one of 'absolute liability' – these are usually less serious regulatory offences.

There is a presumption in criminal law that mens rea is always required. Consequently, if the mens rea is not stated, the court may read (ie infer) a required state of mind into the offence. The wording may make it entirely clear that the offence is one of strict liability. If it does not, consider:

- Where the offence seeks to promote public safety (eg driving and environmental offences), it is more likely to be one of strict liability.
- If the offence targets a group of people obliged to act carefully in order to protect the public from harms arising from tainted food, the sale of drugs and alcohol or are those engaged in industrial activities that pose a danger, then the courts are more likely to find an offence is one of strict liability.
- If the offence will have the effect of encouraging compliance with the law (eg selling lottery tickets to underage persons), it is more likely to be a strict liability offence.

■ KEY POINT CHECKLIST

This chapter has covered the following key knowledge points. You can use these to structure your revision, ensuring you recall the key details for each point, as covered in this chapter.

- Actus reus and mens rea are the building blocks of criminal liability. Both must be proven to the criminal standard for the defendant to be criminally liable.
- Offences can be committed by a failure to act but only where they are capable of being committed by omission and D is under a duty to act.
- For result offences, the defendant must have caused the prohibited result. There are two tests for causation (the factual and the legal test) and both must be satisfied for liability to attach.

- The requisite mens rea must be satisfied for the elements of the actus reus, and the actus reus and mens rea must coincide.
- Intention may be either direct or oblique. Direct intention is where it is the defendant's aim or purpose to bring about the result. Intention may alternatively be found through a direction asking whether the consequence was a virtually certain one and the defendant appreciated such.
- Recklessness is subjective and is where the defendant takes an unjustifiable risk and is aware of that risk.
- Negligence is objective and looks to whether the defendant's conduct falls short of the standard expected by the reasonable person.
- Offences may be strict liability, requiring no mens rea for one or more elements of the actus reus.

■ KEY TERMS AND CONCEPTS

- actus reus (**page 3**)
- mens rea (**page 3**)
- causation (**page 3**)
- direct intention (**page 12**)
- oblique intention (**page 12**)
- transferred malice (**page 17**)

■ SQE1-STYLE QUESTIONS

QUESTION 1

A man stabs a love rival in the stomach and the victim is taken to the hospital. At the hospital, the victim is given antibiotics to prevent infection. Unbeknown to the medical staff, he is allergic to the antibiotics and he swiftly dies. The man is charged with murder.

Has the medical treatment broken the chain of causation?

A. Yes, the medical team have acted negligently, and this breaks the chain of causation.

B. Yes, the treatment was palpably wrong, and this broke the chain of causation.

C. No, the chain of causation has actually been broken by the unanticipated vulnerability of the victim.

D. No, you must take your victim as you find them, and this includes undiagnosed conditions.

E. Yes, this was a voluntary act by the medical staff that breaks the chain of causation.

QUESTION 2

A man is playing with a shotgun that he has discovered at his friend's farmhouse. That evening, the man and his friend get into an argument and he points the gun at his friend's legs, telling him, 'If you don't shut up, I'll blow off your kneecaps.' The argument continues and the man points the gun near his friend and pulls the trigger. The bullet enters his chest and the friend dies immediately. The man says he was simply trying to scare his friend into shutting up. The man is charged with murder and the judge directs the jury that if death or serious injury was a highly probable result of the man's actions, and he appreciated such, then the jury can find he had the necessary intent.

Is the judge's direction correct?

A. Yes, as the direction has been given as an evidential one.

B. Yes, as the jury have been asked to consider whether they thought the result highly probable and then whether the man thought it highly probable.

C. No, the judge should have given the direction as a legal test, that if the jury found the result was highly probable and the man appreciated this that they must find intent.

D. No, the judge has used incorrect terminology. The direction should have been given in terms of virtual certainty.

E. No, the judge has used incorrect terminology. The direction should have been given in terms of virtual certainty and as a legal test.

QUESTION 3

A woman works as a community nurse and one of her clients is an elderly lady. One afternoon, the woman goes on a scheduled visit to her elderly client's house but gets to the house an hour later than arranged. When no one answers the door, she peers through the window and sees her client laying on the kitchen floor. She decides not to do anything as calling the authorities would alert her employers to the fact that she was late. It is later established that her client had fallen and had died later that day of an embolism.

Was the woman under a duty to act?

A. Yes, all persons are under a duty to act to prevent harm from occurring to others.

B. No, as the woman had not created a dangerous situation, she was not under a duty to act.

C. Yes, as the visiting community nurse, the woman had an obligation to discharge her contractual duty.

D. Yes, by virtue of their close relationship, the woman was under a duty to act.

E. No, only immediate relatives are under a duty to act.

QUESTION 4

A woman has a grudge against a co-worker who she is sure has been stealing her lunch from the office fridge. One afternoon she sees her co-worker sitting at his desk eating a yogurt that she had just discovered was missing. Losing her temper, she threw down the stapler she was holding. It bounced off her desk and hit her supervisor in the leg. The woman has been charged with battery. It was accepted she did not intend to apply force to her supervisor, but she is convicted of battery as the magistrates concluded a reasonable person would have seen a risk of force being applied and it does not matter that the woman may not have done.

Did the magistrates approach recklessness correctly?

A. Yes, it would have been obvious to the reasonable person that there was a risk of the stapler hitting someone.

B. No, this was a justifiable risk.

C. Yes, the woman chose to take that risk and the magistrates need only consider whether a reasonable person would also see the risk.

D. No, the focus should be on whether the woman saw a risk of the prohibited result and went on to take that risk.

E. Yes, recklessness can be approached via an objective or a subjective test.

QUESTION 5

A man is involved in a fight with a woman outside a public house. The man throws a large stone in the direction of the woman, intending that the stone will strike the woman. The stone misses the woman and smashes a large window. The man did not intend or foresee the risk that the stone would damage the window. The man is charged with criminal damage of the window.

Is the man guilty of criminal damage?

A. No, the man cannot be liable on the basis that he lacked intention or recklessness as to criminal damage and his intention to strike the woman cannot be transferred to the window.

B. No, the man cannot be liable as the concept of transferred malice only applies to offences against the person.

C. Yes, the man can be liable on the basis that his intention to strike the woman can be transferred to the window, despite the fact that he did not intend nor was he reckless as to damaging the window.

D. Yes, the man can be liable on the basis that the reasonable person would have foreseen the risk that the window would be damaged as a result of the throwing of the stone.

E. Yes, the man can be liable on the basis that breaking the window was a virtually certain result of his conduct and the reasonable man would have appreciated the result as being a virtual certainty.

■ ANSWERS TO QUESTIONS

Answers to 'What do you know already?' questions at the start of the chapter

1) The actus reus of an offence generally refers to the external elements of an offence, those that do not relate to the state of mind of the defendant (or any objective fault requirement).

2) Yes, but the alleged offence must be one capable of being committed by omission and the defendant must be under a duty to act.

3) False. It may break the chain of causation but only when it is an independent and voluntary act by the third party (and palpably bad in the case of medical treatment) or it is an act of the victim that is unreasonable in the circumstances.

4) The jury must be directed in line with the *Woollin* direction and be asked whether death or serious injury is a virtually certain result of the defendant's actions and whether the defendant realised such.

Answers to end-of-chapter SQE1-style questions

Question 1:
  The correct answer was D. Though medical treatment can break the
  chain of causation it must be palpably wrong (not merely negligent,
  so option A is wrong) and be an independent cause of death. Here
  the victim had an undiagnosed vulnerability and the principle is that
  you must take your victim as you find them (therefore option C is
  incorrect). Option B is incorrect as, though the medical treatment may
  be classified as palpably wrong, the option ignores the application
  of the thin skull rule. Option E is wrong as a voluntary act is not
  sufficient for medical negligence to break the chain of causation.

Question 2:
  The correct answer was D. The direction should have been given
  in terms of virtual certainty and as an evidential test. Option A is
  wrong because, while the test is an evidential one, the reference
  to 'highly probable' is wrong. Terms such as 'highly probable' or
  'possible' indicate recklessness, not intention, and should not be used
  in directing a jury (hence options B and C are incorrect). Although
  there has been some debate about whether the direction is legal or
  evidential, it is generally accepted as an evidential test allowing juries
  to 'find' intention, therefore option E is incorrect.

Question 3:
  The correct answer was C. We are not all placed under a duty to
  act (option A is therefore incorrect), but by virtue of her position as
  a community nurse and, specifically, as the nurse to this particular
  client, she was under a duty to act. Option B is wrong as it supposes
  that the creation of a dangerous situation is the only circumstances
  in which the woman could be liable. Option D is incorrect as a mere
  close relationship is not normally sufficient to impose a duty to act.
  Option E also is wrong because it, much like option B, ignores the
  other ways in which a duty to act may arise.

Question 4:
  The correct answer was D. Recklessness is the taking of an
  unjustifiable risk and that is an objective question, but that is not the
  crux of subjective recklessness (so options A, B and C are incorrect).
  The magistrates should have considered whether the woman actually
  saw the risk. There is no discretion here (so option E is incorrect), it
  must be approached in terms of subjectivity.

Question 5:
  The correct answer was A. This was because the man's malice
  against the woman cannot be transferred to the window (therefore

option C is incorrect). Options D and E are incorrect as they suggest the test for both recklessness and virtual certainty is an objective one, asking what the reasonable man would have foreseen. Option B is incorrect as transferred malice is a general principle and is not restricted to offences against the person.

■ KEY CASES, RULES, STATUTES AND INSTRUMENTS

The SQE1 Assessment Specification does not require you to know any case names, or statutory materials, for the topic of actus reus and mens rea.

2

Parties to a crime

■ MAKE SURE YOU KNOW

This chapter will cover the core principles relating to parties to a criminal offence. The scope of parties to a crime includes consideration of principal offenders, secondary parties and the law of joint enterprise. You are required to know all three concepts and be able to apply these legal principles and rules appropriately and effectively to realistic client-based and ethical problems and situations for your SQE1 assessment.

The SQE1 Assessment Specification has not identified that candidates are required to recall/recite any case names, or statutory materials, for the topic of parties to a crime.

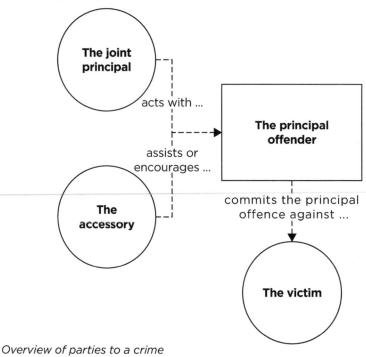

Overview of parties to a crime

■ SQE ASSESSMENT ADVICE

As you work through this chapter, remember to pay particular attention in your revision to:

• the nature of a principal and secondary offender
• the distinction between a principal offender and an innocent agent
• the intention requirement for a secondary party
• the fundamental change in law since the case of *R v Jogee*.

■ WHAT DO YOU KNOW ALREADY?

Have a go at these questions before reading this chapter. If you find some difficult or cannot remember the answers, make a note to look more closely at that area during your revision.

1) What is the difference between a principal offender and an accomplice?

   [Introduction to parties to a crime, pages 28–30]

2) True or false: an accomplice may be liable for an offence in circumstances where he foresees that the principal may commit a particular offence.

   [Intention to assist or encourage and that the principal offence be carried out, pages 35–38]

3) Fill in the blank: in order to determine whether a withdrawal of assistance or encouragement is effective, the jury may take into account _____.

   [Defences to accessorial liability, pages 38–39]

4) What is the difference between accessorial liability and inchoate liability, specifically attempts?

   [Liability of accomplices, pages 30–42]

INTRODUCTION TO PARTIES TO A CRIME

In **Chapter 1**, we focused our attention on the fundamental elements of criminal offences, namely actus reus and mens rea. In that chapter, we focused on the actions of a single defendant acting alone in the commission of an offence. In this chapter, we gain an appreciation as to the other parties that may feature in a criminal offence, specifically secondary parties.

To be well equipped for SQE1, you must understand some of the important terminology used to describe a party, dependent on their contribution to a criminal offence:

* *Principal offender.* A principal offender is the party that commits a substantive criminal offence. This party is the actual perpetrator of the offence in that they have satisfied the necessary actus reus and mens rea of an offence (known as the 'principal offence'). For example:
  - Mark shoots Sam and kills her. Mark is the principal offender for murder.
  - Sam steals a handbag from another. Sam is the principal offender for theft.
* *Joint principal offender.* A joint principal offender is a second party that has equally committed the substantive offence by satisfying the necessary actus reus and mens rea of an offence. For example:
  - Sam and Mark enter the house of another and steal property therein. Both are joint principal offenders for burglary.
  - Mark and Sam attack a man in order to steal his mobile phone. Both kick and punch the man before making off with his phone. Both are joint principal offenders for robbery.
* *Secondary offender.* A secondary offender does not commit the substantive offence (we refer to these parties as 'accessories' or 'accomplices'). The secondary offender has not, by his own conduct, committed the actus reus of the principal offence. Rather, the secondary party has assisted or encouraged the commission of the principal offence. For example:
  - Sam shouts words of encouragement while Mark beats up Adam, causing severe injuries. Sam is not liable for the principal offence, because she has not beaten up Adam, but she can be liable as an accessory for encouraging the principal offence of causing grievous bodily harm (GBH) with intent.
  - Sam intends to set fire to Wayne's house in an act of vengeance. Mark provides Sam with petrol and a lighter. Mark has not taken part in setting the fire, but has aided and abetted the principal offence of arson by providing the petrol and lighter.

For the majority of this revision guide, we focus on a sole principal offender. For the purposes of this chapter, however, we shall focus on the law relating to, and examples of, secondary parties. This has often been referred to as the law of **joint enterprise**.

Key term: joint enterprise

Joint enterprise has been used to describe a multitude of situations involving two or more individuals committing a criminal offence. The term has also been used to refer to those situations where the principal and the accessory intended different results.

Please note that the Supreme Court in *R v Jogee* [2016] UKSC 8 explained that there is no longer any separate category of joint enterprise liability; all cases of assistance or encouragement are to be dealt with using the same principles.

Revision tip

The SQE1 Assessment Specification refers to the law relating to 'accomplices'. This term, however, is interchangeable with 'secondary parties' or 'accessories'. If you come across any of these terms in a multiple-choice question (MCQ), be aware that they relate to the same concept.

Before we proceed to discuss the liability of secondary parties, we need to first consider one final party not considered above, namely that of **innocent agents**.

Key term: innocent agents

An innocent agent is a party who commits the actus reus of a principal offence, following direction from another individual, but, for some reason, they cannot be liable for the offence.

An agent may be innocent because they lack capacity, or they lack the necessary mens rea for the offence. In these circumstances, the acts of the innocent agent can be imputed on to the principal offender. Some examples will assist on the topic of innocent agency:

• Mark intends to kill his partner, Adam. He gives Sam the poison, claiming it was medicine. Sam does not administer the substance, however. Wayne picks up the bottle and unwittingly administers it to Adam, who dies. Mark is the principal offender while Wayne is merely an innocent agent.

- Sam intends to steal a car. She lies to Mark and tells him that the car belongs to her and she needs him to pick it up. Mark does so and unwittingly steals the car. Sam is the principal offender while Mark is merely an innocent agent.

LIABILITY OF ACCOMPLICES

The scope of accessorial liability can be found in s 8 of the Accessories and Abettors Act (AAA) 1861 and can be broken down into four elements, as shown in **Figure 2.1**.

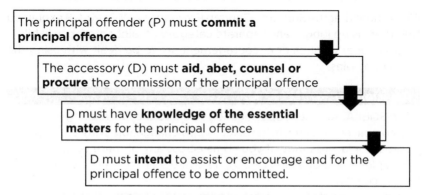

The principal offender (P) must **commit a principal offence**

The accessory (D) must **aid, abet, counsel or procure** the commission of the principal offence

D must have **knowledge of the essential matters** for the principal offence

D must **intend** to assist or encourage and for the principal offence to be committed.

Figure 2.1: Elements of accessorial liability

Exam warning

Do not confuse liability as an accessory with liability for an inchoate offence, such as an attempt considered in **Chapter 3**. Accessorial liability is concerned with the assistance or encouragement provided by D to another person in the commission of an offence. Attempts are concerned with steps taken by D himself to commit an offence. In the former, a full offence is committed, and D is liable for his assistance or encouragement of that offence. In the latter, a full offence has not been committed, and D is liable for the steps he has taken to commit that offence.

If the conditions in s 8 are met, an accessory 'shall be liable to be tried, indicted and punished as a principal offender'.

Commission of a principal offence

The first requirement is that the principal offender must have been successful in their commission of the principal offence. Accessorial liability is 'derivative'; it *derives* from the conduct of the principal. If the principal has not completed an offence, the secondary party cannot be liable as an accomplice. Instead, attention should be focused on the law of inchoate offences (see **Chapter 3**).

Exam warning

Be careful not to misunderstand the nature of a secondary party's liability. Their liability is derived from the *conduct* of the principal offender, not the *guilt/conviction* of the principal offender. If a court is satisfied that the principal offender committed the actus reus of the offence, the secondary party may be liable for their acts of assistance or encouragement. It is irrelevant whether the principal offender is found guilty of the principal offence or not (either because the principal offender may have a valid defence or cannot be found).

There are no restrictions on the type of offences that can be aided, abetted, counselled or procured. While the AAA 1861 applies only to indictable offences (including either way offences), the same provision is made in respect of summary offences by s 44 of the Magistrates' Courts Act 1980.

Revision tip

Always start by identifying whether the actus reus of the principal offence has been committed. Once you have done this, then identify any acts of assistance or encouragement provided by the accomplice.

Aid, abet, counsel or procure

Second, the defendant must either do an act, or fail to do an act where there is a recognised duty to act. This act or omission must *aid*, *abet*, *counsel* or *procure* the principal to commit the offence. Section 8 of the AAA 1861 makes particular reference to the words 'aid', 'abet', 'counsel' and 'procure'. It is evident that Parliament intended to create four separate ways in which the actus reus could be committed; otherwise they would not have used these four separate descriptors.

The meaning of aid, abet, counsel and procure

We shall now consider each term featured in the AAA 1861 (see **Table 2.1**).

Table 2.1: Meaning of aid, abet, counsel and procure

Term	Explanation and examples
Aid	To 'aid' a principal offender is to assist, support or help him to commit the principal offence. For example: • providing the principal with a weapon or equipment to help him commit the principal offence • acting as a lookout.
Abet	To 'abet' a principal offender is to incite, instigate or otherwise encourage him to commit the principal offence. For example: • shouting words of encouragement during the commission of the offence • cheering and applauding another.
Counsel	To 'counsel' a principal offender is to advise or solicit him to commit the principal offence. Importantly, the principal must be aware that he is being encouraged to commit the offence. For example, hiring a hitman to carry out a murder.
Procure	To 'procure' is to 'produce by endeavour' (ie D has caused, in some way, the offence to come about). For example: • lacing the principal offender's drink, knowing that he will drive home intoxicated and commit an offence by doing so • directing your wife to have sex with another person knowing that she does not consent to the sexual intercourse.

As you can see from **Table 2.1**, the words are very similar, often overlapping. As a result of this overlap, the courts appear to have moved away from this statutory phraseology. In the leading case of *R v Jogee*, for example, Lord Hughes explained that the requisite conduct element is that the defendant has 'encouraged or assisted the commission of the offence' by the principal. Therefore, it may be appropriate to refer to this element of the actus reus as being that the defendant must 'assist or encourage' the principal offender.

Now that we understand these words, it is necessary to consider some further matters.

Timing of assistance or encouragement

Assistance or encouragement may take place during the commission of the offence or some time before. A defendant is not liable, however, where his assistance or encouragement is provided subsequent to the commission of an offence (eg to prevent a crime from being discovered).

The relevance of causation

The relevance of causation depends upon the type of act alleged against the defendant.

In respect of aiding, abetting and counselling:
- There is no requirement of causation between the conduct of the accomplice and the act of the principal. For example, it would not be necessary to prove that 'but for Mark shouting words of encouragement, Sam would not have committed the offence'.
- There must, however, be 'some connecting link' between the conduct of the accomplice and the actions of the principal. The focus is whether the encouragement was communicated to the principal (in the sense that it came to the principal's attention). Once it is proven that there is communication, the 'connecting link' is made out.

However, where it is alleged that the accomplice procured the offence, it must be proven that the defendant caused the principal to commit the offence.

The relevance of presence at the scene

Mere presence at the scene of a crime is not an offence. Furthermore, the Supreme Court made clear in *Jogee* that mere presence 'is not necessarily proof of assistance or encouragement; it depends on the facts'. Mere presence at the scene is, however, capable of amounting to *evidence* of assistance or encouragement.

In many cases, a passive presence will not be sufficient for an offence to be made out. There are circumstances, of course, where an individual's non-accidental presence *is* capable of amounting to an act of encouragement. For example, in *R v Clarkson* [1971] 3 All ER 344, the defendant (a soldier in the army) entered a barrack room where he found a woman being raped by fellow soldiers. He did not intervene or protest; he merely remained in the room. The court found that his presence was sufficient to amount to the actus reus for encouragement (though note, he lacked the mens rea for the offence, ie that he intended for his presence to encourage the principals to commit the offence).

Exam warning

When you are considering whether D's presence at the scene is sufficient for encouragement, consider whether D said or did anything during the commission of the offence. Did D intervene to prevent the conduct from continuing, or did he express dissent or opposition to the principal's conduct? Had D contributed to the 'force of numbers in a hostile confrontation', or has he let the principal know that he will be there to provide assistance if required? In essence, you are trying to identify whether D's presence at the scene is sufficient to suggest that D encouraged the principal offence to be committed.

The relevance of association

Much like mere presence, an association between the principal and accessory is neither proof of assistance, nor of encouragement.

Knowledge of the essential matters

The first mens rea requirement is that the accomplice must know the **essential matters** that constitute the offence. 'Essential matters' is understood as knowledge of 'any existing facts necessary for it to be criminal' (per Lord Hughes in *R v Jogee*).

Key term: essential matters

Knowledge of essential matters means that D knew the circumstances which form the actus reus of the principal offence that might be committed, and that the principal would act with the requisite mens rea for the principal offence.

In essence, the defendant must know that the principal will commit both the actus reus and mens rea of the principal offence.

Where the defendant knows the particular offence that will be committed, there is little difficulty in proving this element of the mens rea. For example, suppose that Mark asks Sam to act as a lookout while he breaks into a house to steal jewellery. In this case, Sam clearly knows that Mark is committing an offence of burglary and is assisting him by acting as a lookout. However, some difficulty may arise where the defendant's knowledge is not as clear cut. For example, suppose that Mark asks Sam to act as a lookout. Mark does not inform Sam what he is doing. In this scenario, the questions would become: what does Sam know and what is Sam expected to know?

The case law in this area has provided some guidance and is detailed in **Figure 2.2**.

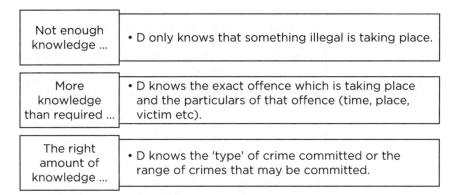

Figure 2.2: Specificity of knowledge for accessorial liability

Table 2.2 (overleaf) explains the phrases 'type' of crime and 'range' of crimes in more detail.

Intention to assist or encourage and that the principal offence be carried out

The final element of the offence is the intention requirement. This element can be broken down into two aspects:

a) The defendant must intend to aid, abet, counsel or procure the principal in committing the offence.

b) The defendant must intend that the principal will act with the necessary mens rea to commit the offence.

Intention to assist or encourage

This first requirement is relatively straightforward: the defendant must provide deliberate (ie intentional) assistance or encouragement to the principal. For example, suppose Mark sells a gun to Sam knowing that she plans to kill her husband with it. Mark may be entirely indifferent to the outcome, but he has deliberately assisted Sam in the commission of the offence.

Table 2.2: Types and ranges of crimes

Principle	Explanation and examples
Type of crime	D need not know the precise details of the crime that was committed but must at least know the *type* of crime that would be committed (eg theft, burglary, unlawful killing). For example, suppose Mark asks Sam to act as a lookout while he is committing a burglary of a particular house. If Mark decides to burgle a different house, Sam is still liable as she is aware of the type of crime being committed.
Range of crimes	Where D contemplates that a range of crimes may be committed, and the principal goes on to commit one of those limited crimes contemplated, D will have the necessary knowledge for the offence. For example, suppose that Sam supplies Mark with a gun. Sam need not know the particular crime that Mark intends to commit with the gun; she may be liable in circumstances where she intentionally assists or encourages Mark to commit one of a range of offences that she has in mind as possibilities (such as robbery, murder or GBH), and Mark commits an offence within that range (eg robbery).

Importantly, only an intention to assist or encourage is sufficient. What about the circumstances where a defendant *foresees* that his conduct may assist or encourage the principal? In *Jogee*, the Supreme Court confirmed that 'foresight may be good evidence of intention but it is not synonymous with it'. On that basis, as discussed in **Chapter 1**, foresight is not equivalent to intention but can be used by the arbiters of fact as *evidence* capable of inferring intention.

Intention that the principal acts with necessary mens rea

If an offence requires a particular intent, the defendant must intend to assist or encourage the principal to act with such intent. For example, the offence of murder requires the principal to intend to kill or cause GBH; an accomplice must therefore intend that the principal will act with either of those intentions.

This element of the offence will cause no difficulties where the principal offence is carried out as intended by the defendant. Difficulties arise, however, where the principal commits an offence unintended by the defendant. As discussed, a mere foresight that the principal might commit a different offence is not the same thing as saying that they intended for the principal to do so. To assist us in this, let us consider two examples.

Practice example 2.1 concerns the circumstances where the principal commits a more serious offence than that intended by the defendant.

Practice example 2.1

Sam and Wayne come to an agreement that they will attack Mark. Their intention is to hurt Mark and to 'teach him a lesson', but they do not intend to cause him really serious harm or death. They only intend 'some harm'. Sam and Wayne attack Mark, with Sam punching Mark in the face and Wayne kicking him. As Sam is about to leave (believing that they have taught Mark a lesson), Wayne pulls out a knife and stabs Mark – killing him in the process. In this case, Sam possesses the actus reus and mens rea for actual bodily harm (ABH) (perhaps GBH), whereas Wayne possesses the actus reus and mens rea for murder. Wayne will be liable for murder.

Is Sam liable for murder in the same way that Wayne is?

In order for Sam to be liable for the more serious offence of murder, Sam would have had to intend for Wayne to kill or cause really serious harm. Therefore, it is likely that the prosecution would charge Sam with murder, with manslaughter as an alternative. If the jury are not sure that Sam intended for Wayne to commit murder, they will acquit Sam of murder, but can still convict her of manslaughter if satisfied that she intended Wayne to commit an unlawful and dangerous act (which they did as they agreed to cause Mark harm, and the reasonable person would consider that to be objectively dangerous – see Chapter 5).

Practice example 2.2 concerns the circumstances where the principal commits a less serious offence than that intended by the defendant.

Practice example 2.2

Sam procures Wayne to scare Mark with a gun. Sam tells Wayne that the gun is loaded with blank ammunition and that he should point the gun at Mark to scare him. Unbeknown to Wayne, the gun is loaded with live ammunition and Sam intends for Wayne to shoot and kill Mark. Wayne shoots Mark and kills him. In this case,

Sam possesses the actus reus and mens rea for murder, whereas Wayne does not possess the mens rea for murder due to his lack of intention. Wayne will be liable for unlawful act manslaughter.

Is Sam liable for manslaughter in the same way that Wayne is?

Given that Wayne does not intend to kill or cause GBH, he cannot be guilty of murder but can be guilty of manslaughter (by unlawful act). Sam, on the other hand, possesses the mens rea for murder and can be liable for the more serious offence of murder despite the fact that Wayne, as the principal, is convicted of a lesser offence.

Defences to accessorial liability

There are a number of defences that specifically apply to those who aid, abet, counsel or procure an offence (in addition to those in **Chapter 4**).

Withdrawal

Where the defendant has a change of heart, and effectively withdraws his assistance or encouragement, he may exceptionally have a defence of withdrawal. This is a decision for the jury who must determine whether the withdrawal was effective in a given case. For example:

- In *R v Grundy* [1977] Crim LR 543, a jury were entitled to find there to be an effective withdrawal where the defendant tried to persuade the principal against committing a burglary two weeks before it took place.
- In *R v Becerra* (1976) 62 Cr App R 212, the defendant jumped out of a window during a burglary when he and the principal were confronted by a householder. The principal would go on to stab the householder with a knife, killing him. The defendant had not effectively withdrawn from the offence by jumping out of the window; he would have had to try to prevent the principal from stabbing the householder in order to effectively withdraw.

To summarise the principles of withdrawal:

- Withdrawal must be communicated through words or conduct unless such communication is impossible (ie there must be some physical action taken to withdraw; mere change of mind or 'failure to show up' is not an effective withdrawal).
- Withdrawal must be an unequivocal disengagement from the criminal enterprise.
- The defendant is not required to have undertaken all reasonable steps in order to withdraw, but there must be a sufficient basis to prove an effective withdrawal.

- In cases where the defendant is involved in spontaneous violence, communication of withdrawal may not be possible or reasonable; he must show disengagement before the offence was committed.
- Withdrawal may take place either before or during the commission of the offence (though more will be required from the defendant to show withdrawal during the commission of the offence, for example physical intervention to prevent the crime from continuing).
- The greater the level of assistance or encouragement, the more work is expected of the defendant to withdraw such assistance or encouragement.

Exam warning

Be aware that while D may avoid liability as an accessory for a successful withdrawal, he may remain liable for an inchoate offence, such as an attempt (see **Chapter 3**). An MCQ may test this knowledge and you must ensure that you are aware of the link between attempts and secondary liability.

Overwhelming supervening event

Where the principal acts in such a manner that 'nobody in the defendant's shoes could have contemplated might happen and is of such a character as to relegate [the defendant's] acts to history', the defendant may not be liable for an offence (*Jogee*). The trial judge would have to be sure that there is an evidential basis for this claim, as opposed to a mere escalation of events that still formed part of the joint enterprise.

For example, suppose Mark acts as a getaway driver for Sam in the commission of a theft. Sam produces a knife and stabs the victim. The jury may be asked to consider whether Sam's production of the knife was an overwhelming supervening event or whether it was simply an escalation of the joint venture.

Outstanding issues in accessorial liability

This chapter has considered some of the fundamental issues in the law relating to accessories. There are some final matters that are worth consideration before we then bring together our understanding of this complex area of law (**Figure 2.3** overleaf).

Uncertainty as to party status

There may be circumstances where there is uncertainty as to whether the defendant was a principal offender or an accessory. So long as a jury is satisfied that the defendant was involved in the commission of a criminal offence, either as a principal or as an accessory, then they may convict on that basis. The jury will first ask whether they are sure that the defendant was a principal; if they are, that is the end of the matter.

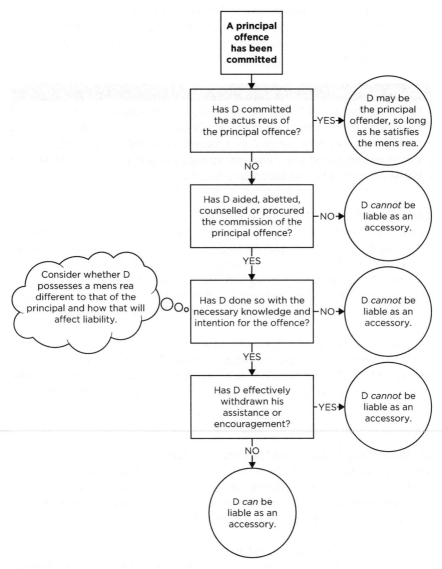

Figure 2.3: Understanding parties to a crime

If they are not sure, they should then ask whether the defendant was an accessory.

Transferred malice

The defendant will not be liable in the circumstances where he and the principal offender have agreed on a particular victim and the principal offender deliberately commits the offence against a different victim.

Relevance of weapons

Knowledge or ignorance on the part of the defendant that the principal is carrying a weapon may be relevant in determining whether he intended the principal to act in a particular way. In *Jogee*, the Supreme Court explained that the presence of weapons carried by the principal is only evidence of the defendant's intention; it is not equivalent to intention (though the court did refer to that inference as potentially 'irresistible').

Conditional intention

A jury may infer an intention to commit an offence in circumstances where the defendant agreed to commit crime A and that crime B may be committed should the occasion arise. For example, suppose Mark and Sam agree to burgle a house, with Sam acting as the lookout. Mark and Sam agree only to steal property from the house and not to disturb the householders, but they also agree that they will cause harm to the householders should the circumstances require it. In this circumstance, the jury may draw the conclusion that Sam has the necessary conditional intent for Mark to cause harm to the householder should the need arise.

Summary: what do we know about parties to a crime?	
Who are the different parties to a crime?	The principal offender is the party who commits the actus reus of the principal offence. They may work with another principal (known as a joint principal). An accomplice/accessory does not commit the actus reus but does aid, abet, counsel or procure the principal(s) to commit the offence. An innocent agent is a party who commits the actus reus of the offence but does not satisfy the mens rea for whatever reason.

What do the words 'aid', 'abet', 'counsel' and 'procure' mean?	These four words are understood to mean that the accessory assists or encourages the principal to commit the offence. Such assistance or encouragement must come before the offence is committed and there is no requirement for a causal link between the offence and the assistance/ encouragement.
What is the mens rea requirement for accessorial liability?	The accessory must intend to assist or encourage, must intend for the principal to act with the necessary mens rea for the principal offence and must know the essential matters of the offence. D may still be liable even if the principal commits a different offence to the one intended.
Might D avoid liability as an accessory?	Yes, if he can demonstrate that he has made an effective withdrawal of his assistance or encouragement from the offence, or where there was an overwhelming supervening event. This is a question of fact and degree for the jury.

■ KEY POINT CHECKLIST

This chapter has covered the following key knowledge points. You can use these to structure your revision, ensuring you recall the key details for each point, as covered in this chapter.

• An accomplice does not commit the actus reus of the principal offence but has assisted or encouraged (aided, abetted, counselled or procured) the commission of the offence.

• The accomplice must intend for the principal to act with the necessary mens rea for that offence. Should the principal commit a crime of greater or lesser severity, the accomplice may still be liable for an offence.

■ KEY TERMS AND CONCEPTS

- joint enterprise (**page 29**)
- innocent agent (**page 29**)
- essential matters (**page 34**)

■ SQE1-STYLE QUESTIONS

QUESTION 1

A man and a woman agree to burgle a house with intention to steal property. The man will enter the property and steal items while the woman will act as a lookout. While in the house, the man is confronted by the householder. The man attacks the householder causing ABH. The man pleads guilty to burglary and assault occasioning ABH, contrary to s 47 of the Offences Against the Person Act 1861, and claims that the woman had accepted that force would be used on the householder if necessary.

Which of the following best describes the liability of the woman?

A. The woman can only be liable for burglary on the basis that she assisted the commission of the burglary; the woman cannot be liable for assault occasioning ABH as she did not agree prior to the burglary to any assault.

B. The woman is liable for burglary as she assisted in the commission of the burglary; the woman can be liable for assisting or encouraging assault occasioning ABH if the jury are sure that the woman intended that the man would, if he thought it necessary, use force on the householder to carry out the burglary.

C. The woman can only be liable for burglary on the basis that she assisted the commission of the burglary; the woman cannot be liable for assault occasioning ABH as the man has gone beyond the plan agreed between himself and the woman and the woman cannot be liable in these circumstances.

D. The woman is liable for burglary as she assisted in the commission of the burglary; the woman can be liable for assisting or encouraging assault occasioning ABH if the jury are sure that the woman foresaw that the man would, if he thought it necessary, use force on the householder to carry out the burglary.

E. The woman is liable for both burglary and assault occasioning ABH as she assisted in the commission of the burglary and the assault was committed while the burglary was taking place.

QUESTION 2

A man and a woman are charged with causing GBH with intent, contrary to s 18 Offences Against the Person Act 1861. The victim suffered a fractured skull caused by a kick to the head. The prosecution allege that both the man and the woman kicked the victim in the head, with intent to cause really serious harm, while the victim was on the ground. The prosecution allege that it was the woman's plan to attack the victim, although they cannot say whether the man or the woman caused the fractured skull but say that each person is guilty either as a principal or an accessory. Each blames the other for the fractured skull.

Which of the following correctly explains the liability of the man and woman?

A. Neither the man nor the woman can be liable for s 18 GBH with intent on account that the prosecution has not alleged which person was the principal and which was the accessory.

B. Both the man and the woman would be liable for s 18 GBH with intent as joint principals. As the prosecution alleges that the man and woman are either a principal or an accomplice, the jury should work on the basis that both the man and the woman are joint principals.

C. Neither the man nor the woman can be liable for s 18 GBH with intent on account that the prosecution has not alleged which person was the principal and which was the accessory. However, both the man and the woman could be liable for s 20 GBH on the basis of the lesser mens rea requirement.

D. The woman can be liable for s 18 GBH with intent as the principal offender as it was her plan to attack the victim; the man can be liable as an accessory to s 18 GBH.

E. Either the man or the woman can be liable for s 18 GBH with intent where the prosecution can prove that they were involved, in some way, with the commission of the offence. It is irrelevant if the prosecution cannot prove that one was the principal and the other the accessory; it is for the jury to make that determination.

QUESTION 3

A farmer instructs his employee to drive a tractor and trailer on a public road as part of his employment. The tractor is poorly maintained, and the employer is aware of this. The employee does as instructed and is involved in a car accident, killing the victim, a passenger in another car, when the trailer becomes detached from the tractor. The employee is charged with causing death by reckless driving but pleads not guilty on account that he was not reckless in his driving due to his lack of knowledge about the dangerous condition of the vehicle.

Which of the following best describes the employer's liability?

A. The employer is liable for procuring the employee to commit death by reckless driving.

B. The employer is only liable for procuring the employee to commit death by reckless driving where the employee has been convicted of the principal offence.

C. The employer is only liable for procuring the employee to commit death by reckless driving where the employee has committed the actus reus of the principal offence.

D. The employer is not liable for procuring the employee to commit death by reckless driving as the employee was obliged by his contract of employment to follow the instructions of his employer.

E. The employer is not liable for procuring the employee to commit death by reckless driving.

QUESTION 4

A woman supplies cutting equipment to a man. The man uses the equipment to break into a bank. The woman admits that she suspected that the equipment would be used for something illegal, such as breaking up stolen goods, but denies that she knew it would be used for committing the offence at that particular bank, on that day and at that time. The prosecution allege that the woman knew that the equipment would be used for a crime of the type committed by the man, or at the very least, it was a crime from a range of offences that she contemplated would be committed.

Which of the following best describes the direction that should be given by the judge to the jury?

A. The woman can be liable if the jury accept that she did know of the existence of some illegal venture.

B. The woman can only be liable if the jury accept that she did know that a particular crime would be taking place, at a particular place and time.

C. The woman can only be liable if the jury accept that she did know that the equipment would be used for the type of crime committed.

D. The woman can be liable if the jury accept that she did know of the type of crime that may be committed, or the range of offences that may be committed.

E. The woman can only be liable where she contemplates a range of offences that may be committed by the man.

QUESTION 5

A man and a woman are involved in a spontaneous fight at a restaurant with the owner of the restaurant. It is unknown as to who initiated the fight. The man attacks the victim with a weapon but soon thereafter drops his weapon and walks away. The woman grabs a knife and stabs the victim to death. The woman is charged with murder and the man is charged with assisting or encouraging the woman to commit murder.

Which of the following best describes whether the man has effectively withdrawn from the offence?

A. The man is unlikely to have effectively withdrawn from the offence. The man would have needed to communicate to the woman that he was disengaging from the offence.

B. The man is unlikely to have effectively withdrawn from the offence. The man would have needed to attempt to prevent the woman from killing the victim in order to effectively withdraw.

C. The man may have effectively withdrawn from the offence. Given that the violence was spontaneous, it would be neither practical nor reasonable to expect the man to communicate his withdrawal to the woman.

D. The man is unlikely to have effectively withdrawn from the offence. A mere change of mind on the man's part was not sufficient; a more physical act of withdrawal was required.

E. The man may have effectively withdrawn from the offence. It was
sufficient for the man to stand to one side to show that he has
withdrawn from the offence.

■ ANSWERS TO QUESTIONS

Answers to 'What do you know already?' questions at the start of the chapter

1) A principal offender commits the actus reus of an offence; an
accomplice does not commit the actus reus but does intentionally
assist or encourage the principal to commit the offence in
question.
2) False. The Supreme Court in *R v Jogee* fundamentally restated the
law in this area, which now requires that the accomplice intended
that the principal would commit the offence with the necessary
mens rea for the offence. Foresight is merely evidence of such
intention.
3) In order to determine whether a withdrawal of assistance or
encouragement is effective, the jury may take into account the time
at which the withdrawal was made in relation to the time when the
offence was committed, the manner in which such withdrawal was
communicated, the steps taken to prevent the crime from being
committed, etc. It is a question of fact and degree for the jury.
4) Accessorial liability concerns the liability of a defendant who assists
or encourages another person to commit an offence. Attempts
concern the situation where the defendant takes his own steps to
commit a criminal offence.

Answers to end-of-chapter SQE1-style questions

Question 1:
The correct answer was B. This is because the woman has actively
assisted in the commission of the burglary by acting as a lookout
and can be liable for ABH if the jury are sure that she intended
for sufficient force for ABH to be used on the householder if
necessary. Option A is incorrect as there is no requirement for prior
agreements in accessorial liability. Option C would be correct if
the woman had not intended for force to be used; however, since
there is evidence that force should be used if necessary, option C is

wrong. Option D is wrong because mere foresight that force may be used is only evidence of intention and is not synonymous with intention. Option E is wrong as it does not accurately describe the fact that the woman had to additionally intend for force to be used if necessary.

Question 2:

The correct answer was E. This is because the prosecution are not required to allege that a defendant was either a principal or an accessory – it is sufficient to prove that a defendant was involved in the commission of the offence in some way (option A is therefore incorrect). If the prosecution was unable to prove any involvement, then neither the man nor the woman could be liable. Option B is incorrect as no such basis for the jury exists in law. Option C is incorrect as it is irrelevant which offence is charged against the man and the woman. Option D is incorrect as simply because the attack was the woman's idea does not mean that she is the principal; whether the woman was a principal offender is determined by whether she caused the fractured skull.

Question 3:

The correct answer was C. This is because the employer will be liable where he has assisted or encouraged the principal to commit the actus reus of the offence. It is irrelevant whether the principal is guilty or not; the liability for the accessory derives from conduct and not from guilt (therefore option B is wrong). While option A is technically correct, it fails to adequately explain why the employer is liable, and thus is not the best description available (it is therefore wrong). Option D is incorrect as it is irrelevant whether the principal was an employee of the accessory and following instructions. Option E is wrong as the employer can be liable for procuring the offence for the reasons stated above.

Question 4:

The correct answer was D. This is because a defendant can be liable in circumstances where they know the type of crime that will be committed following their assistance or encouragement or can contemplate a range of crimes that may be committed. Option A is incorrect on the basis that simple knowledge of some illegal venture is not sufficient knowledge. Option B is wrong on the basis that the woman is not required to know the specifics of the offence being committed. Option C is wrong as it discounts the range of offences contemplated and option E is wrong as it ignores that the woman can be liable if she knows of the type of offence that will be committed.

Question 5:

The correct answer was C. This is because a withdrawal may be made during spontaneous violence without the need for communication where such communication would not be reasonable or practical. This is different in law, and is distinguished in case law, from the situation where the offence has been pre-planned. Furthermore, the fact that there is no evidence that either the man or the woman instigated the fight originally, it is more likely that a court would be sympathetic to the withdrawal of the man (option A is therefore wrong). Option B is incorrect as although a prevention of the offence from being committed would be good evidence of withdrawal, it is not required in all circumstances (all cases must be determined on their own facts). Option D is incorrect as, although a mere change of mind is not sufficient, the man in this case has dropped the weapon and walked away from the violence (he has therefore done some physical act of withdrawal). Option E is incorrect as it is not the best description of when a withdrawal can be made; merely standing to one side is unlikely to be sufficient.

■ KEY CASES, RULES, STATUTES AND INSTRUMENTS

The SQE1 Assessment Specification does not require you to know any case names, or statutory materials, for the topic of parties to a crime. Despite this, you are strongly advised to read s 8 AAA 1861 in full and the associated case law interpreting that statute (especially *R v Jogee*).

3

Inchoate offences

■ MAKE SURE YOU KNOW

This chapter will cover the core principles of inchoate offences. The scope of inchoate offences is wide reaching in criminal law. However, for the purposes of the SQE1 assessment, you are only required to know the law relating to attempts to commit an offence and be able to apply these legal principles and rules appropriately and effectively to realistic client-based and ethical problems and situations.

The SQE1 Assessment Specification has not identified that candidates are required to recall/recite any case names, or statutory materials, for the topic of attempts.

What are inchoate offences?

These are offences which have not yet been completed, but steps have been taken to their commission.

What is an attempt?

An offence in which D intends to commit an offence, but does not satisfy the actus reus of the offence.

Inchoate Offences

Why do we have inchoate liability?

Inchoate offences exist to prevent the commission of criminal offences by criminalising planning and preparation for a criminal offence.

When will D have 'attempted' an offence?

D's conduct must be classed as being 'more than merely preparatory' in order to be criminalised as an attempt.

Overview of inchoate offences and attempts

■ SQE ASSESSMENT ADVICE

As you work through this chapter, remember to pay particular attention in your revision to:

• the fact that an offence can only be attempted if it is an 'indictable' offence
• the circumstances where a court may find a defendant's conduct to be more than merely preparatory
• the strict nature of the mens rea requirement for an attempt.

■ WHAT DO YOU KNOW ALREADY?

Have a go at these questions before reading this chapter. If you find some difficult or cannot remember the answers, make a note to look more closely at that area during your revision.

1) Fill in the blank: an 'indictable offence' is defined as

_____.

   [The offence in question must be one that can be attempted, pages 53–54]

2) An attempt can be committed by an omission. True or false?

   [Commission of an 'act', page 54]

3) Can a defendant be liable for an attempt where the full offence is impossible to commit?

   [Attempting the impossible, pages 57–58]

4) True or false: the mens rea for attempted murder is the intention to kill or cause really serious harm.

   [Intention to commit the full offence, pages 56–57]

INTRODUCTION TO INCHOATE OFFENCES

The term 'inchoate' relates to things that are in development or are not fully formed. The law of inchoate offences is concerned with situations where an individual has not committed a substantive offence but has performed certain preparatory steps for the commission of a substantive offence. A defendant may be liable where he has attempted an offence or conspired with another to commit an offence. As noted at the start of this chapter, *the SQE1 assessment only requires you to know the law relating to attempts.* That shall be the focus of this chapter.

THE OFFENCE OF ATTEMPT

An **attempt** is an offence where a defendant will have taken steps to commit the full offence but is prevented from doing so for some reason. In this circumstance, the defendant possesses the mens rea to commit the full offence, but lacks the necessary actus reus.

Key term: attempt
An attempt is where a person has made an effort to commit an offence but does not successfully complete it.

This failure may come about for a number of reasons, such as:
• the defendant had a change of heart
• the defendant was physically prevented from completing the offence
• the circumstances did not work out as planned by the defendant.

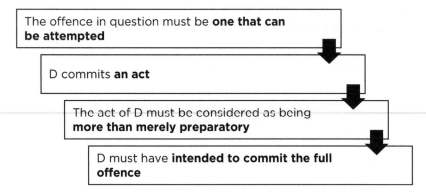

Figure 3.1: Elements of attempt

An example is the case of *R v White* [1910] 2 KB 124, considered in **Chapter 1**. In this case, the defendant added poison to his mother's drink in order to kill her. However, the mother died of natural causes. Here, the defendant could not be liable for murder on account that his unlawful act did not cause the death of the mother, despite his intention to kill. In this circumstance, the more appropriate charge is one of attempted murder.

The offence of attempt is provided for in s 1 of the Criminal Attempts Act (CAA) 1981 and can be broken down into four elements, as shown in **Figure 3.1**.

The offence in question must be one that can be attempted

The first requirement is that the defendant can only be liable for an attempt in circumstances where the offence in question is *capable* of being attempted. An offence can be attempted if it is an 'indictable offence'. **Figure 3.2** provides clarity as to the meaning of an indictable offence.

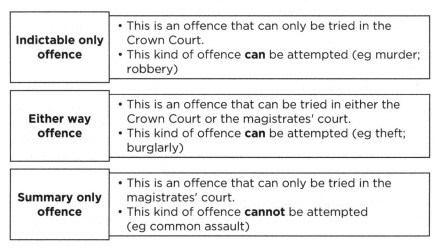

Indictable only offence	• This is an offence that can only be tried in the Crown Court. • This kind of offence **can** be attempted (eg murder; robbery)
Either way offence	• This is an offence that can be tried in either the Crown Court or the magistrates' court. • This kind of offence **can** be attempted (eg theft; burglarly)
Summary only offence	• This is an offence that can only be tried in the magistrates' court. • This kind of offence **cannot** be attempted (eg common assault)

Figure 3.2: Understanding 'indictable' offences

Exam warning

A multiple-choice question (MCQ) may try to test your knowledge as to where the dividing line lies between charging D with a full offence or an attempt. Make sure that you are aware that D cannot be guilty of both an attempt and the substantive offence. The prosecution must decide whether to charge D with the full offence or the attempt. If the prosecution are not satisfied that the full offence has been committed, they will charge an attempt, even if there is evidence to suggest that the full offence has been committed. Look out for claims in the MCQ that D can be liable for both.

In addition, the CAA 1981 identifies a number of statutory exclusions (ie offences that cannot be attempted). These include attempts to:

- commit conspiracy
- aid, abet, counsel or procure
- encourage or assist suicide
- impede an arrest or compound an offence.

Some of these offences were discussed briefly in **Chapter 2**.

Exam warning

Be aware that low-value shoplifting (ie where the value of goods offered for sale in a shop do not exceed £200) is an offence triable only summarily. While summary only offences cannot be attempted, low-value shoplifting is an offence that *is* capable of being attempted. If you come across an MCQ which suggests that D cannot be liable for attempting to steal a £20 steak, as it is a summary only offence, please remember this exception.

Commission of an 'act'

The next point to make is that an attempt can only be committed by an act. This is evident in s 1(1) CAA 1981, which provides that an offence is committed where 'a person does *an act*'. This would suggest that the offence of attempt cannot be committed by omission (see **Chapter 1**).

More than merely preparatory

The core of attempts law revolves around the phrase '**more than merely preparatory**', which is a creation of s 1 CAA 1981.

Key term: more than merely preparatory

The phrase is not defined in the legislation but must be afforded its 'plain natural meaning'. It is usually understood to include the circumstances where D has 'embarked on the crime proper' or has actually tried to commit the offence in question. Where D has merely got ready or put himself in a position or equipped himself to commit the offence, this is unlikely to be sufficient.

Whether the acts are sufficient to be considered as being more than merely preparatory is a question of fact for the jury, so long as the judge is satisfied in law that there is evidence to support that finding (see **Table 3.1** for examples).

Table 3.1: Cases dealing with 'more than merely preparatory'

Facts and principle	More than merely preparatory?
D confronted the victim with a sawn-off shotgun in the victim's car. The victim managed to escape unharmed. While D had a number of further steps to take before he could commit the offence, his conduct was more than merely preparatory. In particular, D had: • entered the victim's car • taken out the gun • pointed the gun at the victim. By taking these steps, D had embarked on the 'crime proper' and it was irrelevant that there were further steps to be taken. *R v Jones* [1990] 3 All ER 886	YES
D stood outside of a sub-post office for 30 minutes wearing a motorcycle helmet and carrying an imitation gun and a threatening note. D never entered the premises and was apprehended a yard from the door to the post office. D's acts were not more than merely preparatory in that he had not gained entry to the sub-post office, nor had he drawn the gun. His actions up to the point of arrest were 'indicative of mere preparation' and could not be classed as more than merely preparatory. *R v Campbell* (1991) 93 Cr App R 350	NO
D was found in the boys' toilet at a school, carrying a rucksack containing a knife, masking tape and rope. D was caught by a member of staff before coming into contact with any children. D had not done an act that was more than merely preparatory on account that he had not 'actually tried to commit the offence in question'. D had merely 'got ready or put himself in a position or equipped himself to do so.' *R v Geddes* [1996] Crim LR 894	NO

As you can see, whether an act is more than merely preparatory is entirely reliant on the facts of any given case. You should familiarise yourself with cases in this area so that you are better placed to identify the factors that suggest the defendant may have 'crossed the line' between merely preparatory steps and *more than* merely preparatory steps.

Revision tip

When considering whether D has done an act that is more than merely preparatory to the commission of an offence, it is worth identifying what the actus reus elements of the substantive offence are and asking, based on those elements, whether D's conduct can be classed as more than merely preparatory to the commission of the full offence. Quite simply, think about whether D has tried to commit any of the actus reus elements of the offence.

Intention to commit the full offence

The final element of this offence is that the defendant must intend to commit an offence. Intention in this context includes both direct and oblique intention (see **Chapter 1**).

In summary, the defendant must intend to commit all of the elements of the offence (ie the actus reus), including an intention that any end result should be manifested (see **Practice example 3.1**). This often means that an attempt can be more difficult to prove than the full offence.

Practice example 3.1

Arthur had administered an electric shock to his wife while she was in the bath. His wife had suffered an electric shock but survived. Arthur was charged with attempted murder. The trial judge directed the jury that they could convict Arthur of attempted murder if they were sure that he intended to kill his wife, or that he intended to cause her grievous bodily harm (GBH). The jury convicted Arthur of attempted murder.

Do you think the trial judge was correct in his directions to the jury?

These were the facts of *R v Whybrow* (1951) 35 Cr App R 141. The Court of Criminal Appeal accepted that there was a misdirection by the trial judge on account that while the level of intention required for murder was an intention to kill or an intention to cause GBH, the offence of attempted murder could only be committed by an intention to kill; an intention to cause GBH is not sufficient for attempted murder.

In summary, it must always be proved that the defendant intended to commit the offence in question, even though the complete offence is one that is capable of being committed recklessly or with an intention to a lesser actus reus. A second example is the case of *R v O'Toole* [1987] Crim LR 759, in which the Court of Appeal quashed a defendant's conviction for attempted arson on account that the trial judge directed the jury to consider whether the defendant was reckless as to causing damage by fire. The Court of Appeal made clear that while the full offence may be committed by either intention or recklessness as to the damage being caused by fire, an attempt can only be committed with an *intention* to commit the full offence (ie an *intention* to cause damage by fire). **Figure 3.3** demonstrates this point.

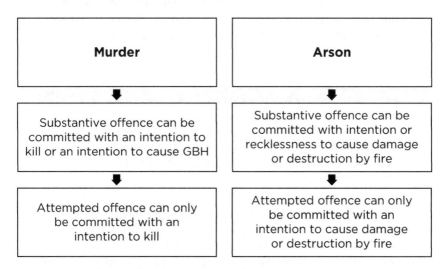

Figure 3.3: Understanding the mens rea of attempts

Attempts, impossibility and withdrawal
The final matter to consider is whether the defendant can avoid liability in circumstances where the offence he attempted was 'impossible' to commit, or where he withdraws from an attempt.

Attempting the impossible
A defendant can still be liable for an attempt even in circumstances where the commission of the offence would be *factually* impossible. For example:

• Mark intends to kill Sam by stabbing her. Mark believes that Sam is asleep and stabs her in the throat. In fact, Sam had already died from natural causes. In this case, the offence is factually impossible to commit (ie you cannot kill someone who is already dead). However, this factual impossibility will not prevent Mark from being liable for attempted murder.

A further form of factual impossibility is known as impossibility by 'inadequate means', in which an offence is both factually and legally possible, but the offence is not committed due to ineptitude or other reasons. For example:

- Sam tries to poison Mark by placing the poison into his coffee in order to kill him. The offence is both factually and legally possible. However, the substance Sam places into the coffee is not poison at all; the substance is perfectly harmless. In this situation, Sam remains liable for the attempted murder of Mark even though the substance was harmless.

Exam warning

Be aware that factual impossibility is judged according to facts as D believes them to be (eg D believes his wife to be alive, even though she is not). An MCQ may try to suggest that this is not the case, or may test your knowledge or understanding about this generally.

However, s 1(2) only provides that *factual* impossibility is no defence. If a defendant attempts something which is *legally* impossible in England and Wales, there can be no liability. For example:

- Homosexual relations are illegal in a man's home country. The man arranges to meet with another adult man in England and engage in sexual intercourse. However, the man loses the courage to do so and does not go to the agreed location. In this case, homosexual relations are not illegal in England and Wales. It is legally impossible for the man to commit an offence; it is therefore legally impossible for him to attempt to commit an offence.

Figure 3.4 (overleaf) provides a summary of attempt and impossibility.

Withdrawal

No defence of 'withdrawal' exists for the offence of attempt as it does in cases of secondary liability considered in **Chapter 2**. This is because attempts involve actions that are more than merely preparatory. Once those actions have been committed, the offence of attempt has been committed, and there is no window for a withdrawal.

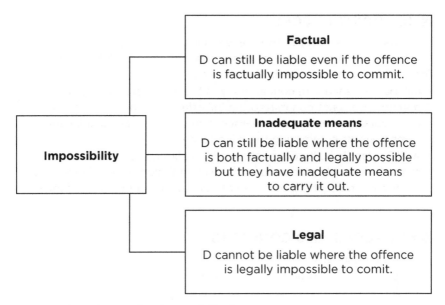

Figure 3.4: Understanding impossibility in attempts

Summary: what do we know about inchoate offences and attempts?	
What offences can be committed by an attempt?	Any indictable offence can be attempted, with a number of notable exceptions.
What is the meaning of 'more than merely preparatory'?	D must have done an act that was more than mere preparation towards the commission of the offence. D must have taken sufficient steps towards committing the offence, but falls short of the full offence.
What is the mens rea requirement for attempts?	D must intend all of the elements of the offence, even if the substantive offence can be committed with a lesser mens rea.
Is impossibility a defence to attempt?	Factual impossibility (including inadequate means) are not 'defences' to an offence of attempt. However, D is not capable of attempting an offence that is legally impossible.

■ KEY POINT CHECKLIST

This chapter has covered the following key knowledge points. You can use these to structure your revision, ensuring you recall the key details for each point, as covered in this chapter.

- Inchoate offences are concerned with the circumstances where a defendant has not committed the full offence. It ensures that the defendant's conduct is criminalised when he has taken significant steps towards committing the full offence.
- A defendant is guilty of an attempt if he commits an act that is more than merely preparatory to the commission of an offence. The defendant must intend to commit the actus reus of the full offence.

■ KEY TERMS AND CONCEPTS

- attempt (**page 52**)
- more than merely preparatory (**page 54**)

■ SQE1-STYLE QUESTIONS

QUESTION 1

A woman enters a supermarket with the intention to steal. The woman picks up a £50 bottle of whiskey and places it into her handbag. The woman is immediately stopped by store security. The supermarket is concerned that the woman will not be convicted of theft and wonders whether the woman could be guilty of attempted theft.

Is the woman likely to be guilty of attempted theft?

A. No, the woman has attempted to commit low-value shoplifting, which is a summary only offence and cannot be attempted.

B. Yes, the woman has attempted to commit theft, which is an either way offence and can be attempted.

C. No, the woman's action of placing the whiskey in her handbag is not an act that is more than merely preparatory in the commission of the offence and cannot amount to an attempt.

D. Yes, the woman has attempted to commit low-value shoplifting and, while it is a summary only offence, it can be attempted.

E. No, the woman has attempted to commit theft, which is a summary only offence and cannot be attempted.

QUESTION 2

A man has separated from his wife. He has recently become distressed by the fact that his wife has started dating another person ('the boyfriend'). The man goes to the boyfriend's house with the intention to cause him GBH. The man breaks into the house and sees the boyfriend sat in the corner of the room reading a book. The man begins to walk towards him with a hammer in his hand. When the boyfriend sees the man with the hammer raised above his head, he suffers from a heart attack and dies immediately. The man runs from the home but is apprehended by the police shortly thereafter.

Is the man likely to be guilty of an attempt?

A. Yes, the man can be guilty of attempted murder as he intended to cause GBH to the boyfriend. His actions of breaking into the home and walking towards the boyfriend with a hammer in his hand are acts that are more than merely preparatory to the commission of an offence.

B. No, the man cannot be guilty of attempted murder or attempted GBH to the boyfriend as he has not committed any positive act that is more than merely preparatory to the commission of an offence.

C. Yes, the man can be guilty of attempted GBH to the boyfriend. His actions of breaking into the home and walking towards the boyfriend with a hammer in his hand are more than merely preparatory to the commission of an offence. The man cannot be guilty of murder as he lacked the intention to kill the boyfriend.

D. No, the man cannot be guilty of attempted murder or attempted GBH to the boyfriend as he has not made any physical contact with the boyfriend. In order for an act of attempted murder or attempted GBH to be met, there must at least be some physical contact.

E. Yes, the man can be guilty of attempted murder as he intended to cause GBH to the boyfriend. His actions of breaking into the home and walking towards the boyfriend with a hammer in his hand are acts that are more than merely preparatory to the commission of an offence. The man cannot be guilty of attempted GBH as the boyfriend has died.

QUESTION 3

A man is arrested by customs officials at an airport. The customs officials are suspicious that he is attempting to import illegal substances into the UK. The man believes that his suitcase contains prohibited drugs. Unbeknown to the man, the suitcase contains no illegal substances.

Is the man likely to be guilty of an attempted offence?

A. No, given that he was never in possession of prohibited drugs, the offence could not factually be committed and so the man cannot be guilty.

B. Yes, on account that factual impossibility is no defence to an offence of attempt. It is irrelevant whether the substance was unlawful, the focus is on whether the man believed the substance to be unlawful.

C. No, because the offence was legally impossible to commit given that the man was never in possession of prohibited drugs.

D. Yes, on account that while the offence is not legally possible to commit, it is factually possible and that is sufficient for an attempt.

E. No, because the substance was not a prohibited drug, the man has not done an act that was more than merely preparatory.

QUESTION 4

Late at night, a man was caught by a police officer at a house, standing in front of a damaged front door. The door's locks and hinges had been broken and the door was held by a single bolt at the top. The prosecution alleged that the man had approached the door, inspected it and then damaged the door, with an intention to enter the house as a trespasser and steal property therein, and thus charged him with attempted burglary.

Was the prosecution correct to charge the man with attempted burglary?

A. No, there was no evidence open to the jury that the man intended to steal property in the house.

B. No, there was no evidence open to the jury that the man had done an act that was more than merely preparatory towards the offence of burglary. The man would have had to enter the house in order for his conduct to be classified as more than merely preparatory.

C. Yes, there was evidence open to the jury that the man had done an act that was more than merely preparatory towards the offence of burglary. The man did not have to enter the house in order for his conduct to be classified as more than merely preparatory.

D. No, the man cannot be charged with attempted burglary as the offence was factually impossible given that the man was caught by a police officer.

E. Yes, the man was liable for the offence of attempted burglary at the point that he allegedly inspected the door. All actions that followed that inspection of the door were merely supplementary.

QUESTION 5

A man enters a greengrocer with the intention to steal money from the store. The man is intercepted by the grocer, who lives above the store, before he is able to steal anything. The man is arrested and charged with attempted burglary. The prosecution allege that the man had entered the premises as a trespasser 'with intent to steal therein'. The trial judge withdraws the case from the jury on account that a 'conditional' intent to steal is not sufficient for attempted burglary.

Was the trial judge right to withdraw the case from the jury?

A. No, the prosecution's case was properly stated on the basis that the man's intention was to steal anything of value. A conditional intent is sufficient for attempted burglary.

B. Yes, the prosecution are required to allege that the man intended to steal particular items of property. A conditional intent is not sufficient for attempted burglary.

C. Yes, the phrase 'with intent to steal therein' is too general. While particular pieces of property need not be identified, the prosecution is not permitted to allege particulars that are so general in nature.

D. Yes, the man clearly identified that he intended to steal 'money'. As such, the indictment should have specifically alleged that the man intended to steal any money that he found in the house.

E. No, whether the man possessed the intention to steal any property in the house is a matter of fact for the jury and the judge is not permitted to withdraw a case from them in those instances.

■ ANSWERS TO QUESTIONS

Answers to 'What do you know already?' questions at the start of the chapter

1) An indictable offence is one that can either be tried solely in the Crown Court, or can be tried in either the Crown Court or the magistrates' court. An offence that can only be tried in the

magistrates' court is not an indictable offence and therefore cannot be attempted.

2) While the law is not clear on this point, the answer is likely to be false because the CAA 1981 makes particular reference to the fact that a defendant 'does an act'.

3) This depends on whether the substantive offence is factually or legally impossible. If it is factually impossible, a defendant can still be liable for an attempt. However, if the offence is legally impossible (ie there is no criminal offence), then the defendant cannot be liable for an attempt.

4) False. An attempt requires the intention to commit the 'full offence'. The full offence of murder is to kill another, therefore the only acceptable mens rea is the intention to kill. Attempted murder is technically, therefore, a more difficult offence to prove than murder itself.

Answers to end-of-chapter SQE1-style questions

Question 1:

The correct answer was D. This is because low-value shoplifting can be attempted, despite being a summary only offence (thus option A is incorrect). While option B is technically correct (thus option E is incorrect), the facts of this case would be considered as low-value shoplifting and thus option D is a more accurate statement of law. Given that theft is technically complete when the property is 'appropriated', the woman has done an act that is more than merely preparatory to the commission of theft (so option C is incorrect).

Question 2:

The correct answer was C. This is because the man has done an act of walking towards the boyfriend with a hammer in his hand and has raised the hammer above his head (thus, option B is incorrect). This action is more than merely preparatory to the commission of GBH, for which he had the intention. The man cannot be guilty of attempted murder as he did not intend to kill the man (so option A is incorrect). Option D is incorrect as there is no formal requirement that physical contact is made (though it may be relevant to determining whether the conduct was more than merely preparatory). Option E confuses the law of attempts and intention and is incorrect.

Question 3:

The correct answer was B. This is because factual impossibility is no defence to a charge of attempt (thus, option A is incorrect).

Options C and D are incorrect because the offence is legally possible to commit and option E is irrelevant as it ignores the operation of factual impossibility.

Question 4:

The correct answer was C. This is because the offence of burglary requires that the man enter a building or part of a building as a trespasser. By damaging the door, a jury could be sure that the man intended to enter the building as a trespasser with the intention to steal, cause GBH or do unlawful damage therein. Given that the full offence of burglary is made out at point of entry into the building, the man need not enter the building to be liable for an attempt (so option B is incorrect). On the other hand, the mere inspection of the door would not be sufficient and would be considered 'merely preparatory' (so option E is wrong). Option A is incorrect on account that the jury would be entitled to reach that conclusion based upon all of the evidence in the case. Option D is incorrect on account that it is a misunderstanding of factual impossibility.

Question 5:

The correct answer was A. This is because the prosecution are entitled to draft the indictment broadly to encompass the circumstances where the man has a conditional intention to steal anything of value from the property. There is no requirement to specify what the man attempted to steal (and therefore option B is incorrect). Options C and D are incorrect on the basis that the prosecution do not require specific property to be identified; a conditional intention to steal anything of value is sufficient. Option E is wrong on account that the trial judge is permitted to withdraw cases from the jury where he is satisfied that there is no evidence that the jury could conclude that the man attempted the offence in question. Here, there was ample evidence in any event.

■ KEY CASES, RULES, STATUTES AND INSTRUMENTS

The SQE1 Assessment Specification does not require you to know any case names, or statutory materials, for the topic of attempts. Despite this, you are strongly advised to read s 1 CAA 1981 in full and the associated case law interpreting that statute.

4

General defences

■ MAKE SURE YOU KNOW

This chapter will cover the core principles of general defences in criminal law. General defences are quite extensive in criminal law, however for the purposes of the SQE1 assessment, you are only required to know the law relating to intoxication and self-defence. You are required to apply these legal principles and rules appropriately and effectively to realistic client-based and ethical problems and situations for your SQE1 assessment.

The SQE1 Assessment Specification has not identified that candidates are required to recall/recite any case names, or statutory materials, for intoxication or self-defence.

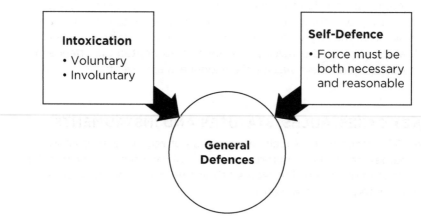

Intoxication
• Voluntary
• Involuntary

Self-Defence
• Force must be both necessary and reasonable

General Defences

Overview of general defences

■ SQE ASSESSMENT ADVICE

As you work through this chapter, remember to pay particular attention in your revision to:

• the effect of a general defence on an individual's liability
• the circumstances in which intoxication can be used as a defence to criminal liability
• why the distinction between specific- and basic-intent offences is important
• the requirements to be proved in order for self-defence to be effective.

■ WHAT DO YOU KNOW ALREADY?

Have a go at these questions before reading this chapter. If you find some difficult or cannot remember the answers, make a note to look more closely at that area during your revision.

1) What are the differences between the following terms: 'general defence', 'special defence', 'complete defence' and 'partial defence'?

   [Introducing general defences, pages 68–70]

2) What is a 'basic-intent offence' and what is a 'specific-intent offence'?

   [Intoxication, pages 70–75]

3) Fill in the blank: 'Proportionate force' means _____.

   [Self-defence/defence of another, pages 75–86]

4) True or false: a defendant who makes a mistake as to whether force is necessary, and that mistake is induced by intoxication, can rely on self-defence.

   [Self-defence/defence of another, pages 75–86]

INTRODUCING GENERAL DEFENCES

Throughout **Chapters 1-3**, we have focused on the core principles of criminal liability in respect of the definitions of offences. In particular, we have identified that the core nature of criminal liability is that the defendant must satisfy both the actus reus and mens rea of an offence (see the figure on **page 1** in **Chapter 1**). However, it is now appropriate to consider some of the circumstances in which a defendant may avoid criminal liability through the operation of a 'defence'. The figure on **page 1** has been revised to incorporate the additional requirement that there must be an absence of a defence to establish liability in **Figure 4.1**.

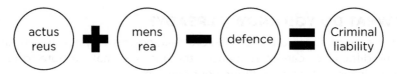

Figure 4.1: Overview of criminal liability (revised)

When charged with a criminal offence, a defendant has a number of options available to him:

- *Plead 'guilty'.* If the defendant pleads guilty, he is accepting the factual basis upon which the prosecution alleges that an offence has been committed.
- *Plead 'not guilty', argue no involvement.* If the defendant pleads not guilty and argues that he had no involvement in the offence, he is disputing the factual basis upon which the prosecution have brought their case. In particular, the defendant is claiming that someone, other than himself, has committed this offence. The defendant will often attempt to rely on an alibi to corroborate his claim that he was not involved in the commission of the offence.
- *Plead 'not guilty', argue a defence.* If the defendant pleads not guilty and argues that he has a defence available to him, he is accepting that he was involved in the commission of the alleged criminal offence but that he has some form of defence which may justify or excuse his liability. In essence, the defendant is claiming that he should not be guilty of an offence because of the operation of a defence.

Our focus in this chapter is where a defendant raises a defence to criminal liability.

Nature of criminal defences

Criminal defences are capable of being categorised in a number of different ways (see **Figure 4.2**).

| General | Specific | Complete | Partial |
| Applies to all offences | Applies to only some offences | Rids D of liability | Reduces D's liability |

Figure 4.2: Comparing the classification of defences

Some examples will assist on this point:
- *Intoxication.* Intoxication is a specific defence as it only applies to specific-intent offences and is also a partial defence in that a successful plea of intoxication will only result in a not guilty verdict for that offence charged. If a lesser offence is available, for which intoxication cannot be a defence, the defendant will be liable for that offence.
- *Self-defence.* Self-defence is a general defence in that it is capable of acting as a defence to all crimes and also acts as a complete defence in that a successful plea of self-defence will result in a not guilty verdict, with the defendant not being liable for any lesser offences.

Burden of proof

In general, the prosecution bears the burden of proving that the defendant committed the offence in question, including the requirement to disprove any defence (this is known as the 'legal burden' – *Woolmington v DPP* [1935] AC 462). The prosecution must discharge this burden 'beyond a reasonable doubt' or so that the jury is 'sure'.

Should a defendant wish to argue a defence, he must raise sufficient evidence to demonstrate that the defence is capable of being argued (this is known as the 'evidential burden'). The defendant is not generally required to prove that the requirements for the defence have been satisfied; their role is to merely provide evidence to support the existence of the defence and make the issue 'live' before the jury. Exceptionally, the defendant may bear a reversed legal burden to prove that a particular defence has been made out. For example, the partial defence of diminished responsibility (see **Chapter 5**) involves a reverse legal burden, requiring the defendant to prove the existence of the defence. Neither intoxication nor self-defence include a reversed burden of proof.

INTOXICATION

It is technically incorrect to refer to **intoxication** as a 'defence'. Rather, intoxication is an argument made by the defendant that, as a result of his intoxicated state, he could not form the necessary mens rea for the offence in question. If the prosecution fails to prove that he held the necessary mens rea for the offence, he cannot be liable. If the defendant possessed the mens rea, despite the intoxication, he remains liable for an offence and cannot argue that he was intoxicated: a drunken intent is still an intent (*R v Sheehan* (1974) 60 Cr App R 308).

Key term: intoxication

Intoxication refers to the situation where D is either drunk, due to the consumption of alcohol, or is inebriated due to the taking of drugs.

While this fundamental basis is simple, the operation of the principle is more challenging. The nature of intoxication as a defence will vary depending on a number of factors:
• whether the defendant was voluntarily or involuntarily intoxicated
• whether the defendant is charged with a basic-intent or specific-intent offence
• whether the intoxicating substance is considered as being dangerous or non-dangerous.

Figure 4.3 (overleaf) provides an overview of how to deal with the issue of intoxication.

Our discussion is best broken down into 'voluntary' and 'involuntary' intoxication, and therein we will discuss the other relevant factors.

Voluntary intoxication

Voluntary intoxication refers to the situation where a defendant has taken an intoxicating substance knowingly and intentionally, for example:
• drinking a pint of beer knowing it is alcoholic (even where you do not realise its strength)
• smoking marijuana knowing it is a drug
• taking LSD.

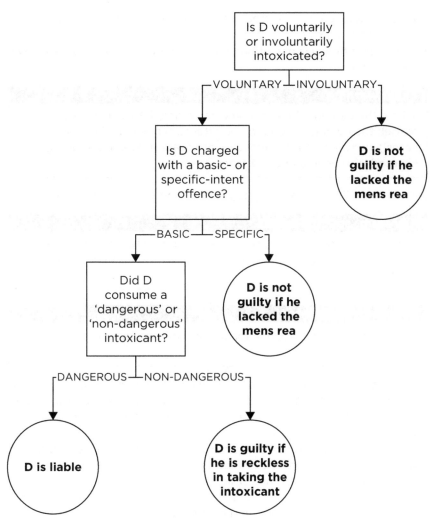

Figure 4.3: Dealing with the rules of intoxication

Stage 1: identify the type of offence

The operation of the defence of voluntary intoxication is entirely reliant upon whether the offence charged is categorised as one of **specific** or **basic intent**. These are known as the Majewski Rules (*DPP v Majewski* [1977] AC 443). These establish that:

• if the offence is one of specific intent, the defendant will have a defence of intoxication where they have been unable to form the necessary mens rea for the offence (it is for the prosecution to prove

that the defendant possessed the relevant mens rea despite being intoxicated); and
- where the offence is one of basic intent, no defence of intoxication will be available.

Exam warning

Where the defendant has become voluntarily intoxicated to give himself the courage to commit an offence (known as 'Dutch courage cases'), he will have no defence of intoxication, even if the offence charged is a specific-intent offence.

All criminal offences can be categorised in one of these two ways.

Key term: specific intent

A specific-intent offence is one for which the defence of intoxication is available so long as D lacks the mens rea for the offence as a result of the intoxication.

Key term: basic intent

A basic-intent offence is one for which the defence of intoxication is unavailable.

So how do we decide whether any given offence is one of specific or basic intent? This has been a matter for the courts, who have developed a number of tests for discerning whether an offence is one of specific intent:

- *Ulterior intent.* Where the mens rea of the offence goes beyond the actus reus, then the offence is one of specific intent (also known as 'ulterior intent'). For example, aggravated criminal damage requires proof that the defendant intended or was reckless as to endangering life. There is no requirement in the actus reus, however, for life to actually be endangered. Aggravated criminal damage is thus an ulterior-intent offence.
- *Purposive intent.* Where the offence requires proof of a 'purposive element', it will be a specific-intent offence. This has normally been understood to mean that the offence is one that can only be committed intentionally (or where the 'predominant' mens rea is intention). For example, murder is an offence that requires an intention to kill or an intention to do serious harm; recklessness will not suffice.

A basic-intent offence would then include crimes of recklessness, negligence or strict liability.

> **Revision tip**
>
> Keep the rules of voluntary intoxication simple in your mind:
> - voluntary intoxication + basic-intent offence = no defence
> - voluntary intoxication + specific-intent offence = defence, so long as D lacks mens rea.

The rationale for disallowing the defence for basic-intent offences is that the defendant will have been reckless in getting himself into that state of voluntary intoxication. This recklessness is then used in place of the mens rea for that offence (see **Figure 4.4**).

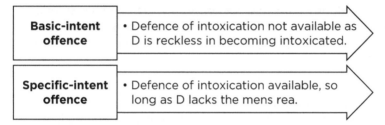

Figure 4.4: The Majewski rules

Stage 2: identify the type of intoxicant
The law draws a distinction between **dangerous drugs** and **non-dangerous drugs**.

> **Key term: dangerous drugs**
>
> Dangerous drugs include alcohol and illegal drugs such as heroin, ecstasy, cocaine and marijuana. When these are ingested, the available defence will be that of intoxication.

> **Key term: non-dangerous drugs**
>
> Non-dangerous drugs are not clearly defined in law and have been variously described as those where the effect of taking them is widely understood to be soporific or sedative, or where the drugs are prescription medication. This is the case even if the prescription is not D's own.

If an intoxicant is considered dangerous, the above rules apply (ie intoxication can be a defence to specific-intent offences but not a defence to basic-intent offences). The rules relating to non-dangerous drugs are more complex and reflect the rules of automatism (a separate defence not featured in the SQE1 Assessment Specification):

• *Specific intent.* Where non-dangerous drugs are voluntarily taken, the defendant will have a defence to a specific-intent offence if he has suffered a total loss of bodily control (ie he is not consciously performing the actus reus).

• *Basic intent.* Where the defendant has been charged with a basic-intent offence, whether he has a defence turns on whether he has been reckless when ingesting the drug – whether he had appreciated it would have such a detrimental impact upon him and that it would make him 'aggressive, unpredictable or uncontrolled' (*R v Bailey* [1983] 2 All ER 503). If he did not appreciate such, and has suffered a total loss of bodily control, he will have a defence. If he was reckless in his consumption of the non-dangerous drug, no defence is available.

Involuntary intoxication

Involuntary intoxication refers to the situation where a defendant has, without will or conscious control, ingested an intoxicating substance. For example, a defendant will be involuntarily intoxicated when

• his drink is spiked with alcohol or drugs

• he ingests non-dangerous drugs in line with medical advice.

It is irrelevant whether the offence charged is one of basic or specific intent – the defence can be utilised in both circumstances (with the exception of strict liability offences). However, the effect of the intoxicant must be that the defendant has been unable to form the mens rea for the offence charged (as with voluntary intoxication) (see **Practice example 4.1**).

Practice example 4.1

Charlie is involved in a business dispute with Vernon. He is aware that Vernon has a sexual predilection for teenage boys and decides to exploit this in order to blackmail him. One afternoon he brings Simon, a 15-year-old boy, to Vernon's hotel room. Both Vernon and Simon have been secretly drugged by Charlie. Vernon goes on to sexually assault Simon while Simon is unconscious. Vernon claims that, although he did intend to touch Simon, he did so only because his inhibitions had been lowered by the intoxicant.

Does Vernon have a defence of involuntary intoxication?

This example is based on the facts of *Kingston* [1995] 2 AC 355. On the facts, Vernon is involuntarily intoxicated, however he has still formed the necessary mens rea for the offence of sexual assault in that he intended to touch Simon. The fact that his inhibitions were lowered by a drug being administered to him does not change that fact. Vernon remains liable for the offence and does not have a defence of intoxication.

Intoxicated mistakes

An honest mistake may ordinarily relieve a defendant of liability. However, where that mistake is induced as a result of the defendant's intoxicated state, the defendant cannot rely on mistake as a defence (though see the exceptional case of *Jaggard v Dickinson* [1981] QB 527, considered in **Chapter 9**).

Revision tip

Keep the rules of involuntary intoxication simple in your mind:

involuntary intoxication + any type of offence = defence, so long as D lacks mens rea.

Summary: what do we know about intoxication?

What are the two types of intoxication?	*Voluntary intoxication*: where D voluntarily consumes drink or drugs, knowing that he is consuming such drink or drugs.
	Involuntary intoxication: where D has not voluntarily ingested the intoxicating substance.
When is the defence of intoxication available?	*Voluntary intoxication*: where D has been charged with a specific-intent offence and the intoxication has negated the mens rea.
	Involuntary intoxication: where the intoxication has negated the mens rea. The type of offence is irrelevant.

SELF-DEFENCE/DEFENCE OF ANOTHER

A defendant charged with a violent offence may seek to argue that he was justified in acting as he did in order to:
• protect himself or another
• protect his property
• prevent a crime or to make a lawful arrest.

The requirements for self-defence are demonstrated in **Figure 4.5**.

> The use of force by D was **necessary** in the
> circumstances as D believed them to be

> The use of force by D was **reasonable** in all
> the circumstances as D believed them to be

Figure 4.5: Elements of self-defence

Please note that while the defendant must raise sufficient evidence of self-defence, it is not for the defendant to prove these elements. Rather, it is for the prosecution to disprove the existence of these elements.

Force is necessary in the circumstances

The first matter to address is whether the defendant believed that it was necessary to use force in a given situation. The necessity to use force may arise from a need to protect oneself or another from an imminent attack, to protect property or to prevent crime. This means that if the use of force was not necessary for any of those reasons (ie it is unjustified), the defence will fail.

Exam warning

Be aware that MCQs commonly try to suggest that self-defence does not extend to the defence of another or the protection of property. Keep in your mind that 'self-defence' is simply an umbrella term to describe the defence of oneself, another or property.

Necessity to use force is a subjective question that looks to the circumstances as the defendant believed them to be. Given that the question is subjective, there are a number of observations that can be made about this first element of the test (see **Table 4.1** overleaf)

Practice example 4.2

Ted saw Asif strike a youth and wrestle him to the ground. Ted intervened in order to protect the youth and, in the process, punched Asif to save the young man from suffering further harm. It was later established that Asif had seen the youth steal a woman's handbag and had been seeking to retrieve the bag and take the man to the police station. Ted has been charged with assault and argues that he was acting in defence of the youth, as he had believed he was under attack.

Could Ted's use of force be viewed as necessary in the circumstances?

This example is based upon the facts of *R v Williams (Gladstone)* [1987] 3 All ER 411. The Court of Appeal made clear that a mistaken but honest belief can form the basis of a self-defence plea as D must be judged 'according to his mistaken view of the facts' even if – objectively – it was an unreasonable mistake to make. If the mistake were an unreasonable one, a jury may find that it was not honestly held.

Table 4.1: Determining whether self-defence was necessary

Factor relevant to the question of necessity	Explanation and examples
Mistaken beliefs	D can rely on a belief that force was necessary in the circumstances even where that belief is mistaken (though see intoxicated mistakes, below). The belief, albeit mistaken, must be genuinely held (see **Practice example 4.2**).
Unreasonable beliefs	D's belief as to the necessity to use force does not need to be reasonable; it must merely be genuinely held. Likewise, any mistaken belief in the need to use force does not need to be reasonable. However, the reasonableness of the belief can be used to determine whether the belief was genuinely held or not (ie the more unreasonable a belief, the less likely it will have been genuinely held).
Intoxicated mistakes	D cannot rely on a mistake about the need to use self-defence where that mistake is induced by D's voluntary intoxication. This is the case even where the offence charged is one of specific intent (NB this exclusion only applies to mistakes induced by *voluntary* intoxication). A defendant may rely on a genuine belief in the need to use self-defence if that has resulted from a mental illness caused by the long-term use of alcohol, however.

Mistake and the defendant's conditions

There is a limit on how far the courts have been prepared to allow the defendant's subjective estimation of the need to use force. For example, while the courts will take into account a defendant's physical conditions (such as age and frailty) when considering whether there was a necessity to use force, the courts are less willing to do so in respect of psychiatric conditions. Where the defendant is suffering from a psychiatric condition (eg delusion beliefs), his estimation of whether there is a need to use self-defence may be affected by that condition. The courts have held that where the condition provides 'strong evidence' of the defendant's honest belief in the necessity to use force, it is relevant. A mistake of fact, based on a delusion caused by mental illness, therefore, can satisfy the first element of the test. There is no guidance on what amounts to 'strong evidence'.

Further issues in self-defence

There are additional matters that may impact upon whether it was necessary to use force, for example:

- *Can you make a pre-emptive strike?* Yes, a pre-emptive strike does not rule out the defence, but the defendant must apprehend that force will be used against him imminently.
- *Can you use force if you had an opportunity to retreat?* Yes, there is no duty to retreat. It is, however, a factor that can be taken into account when deciding whether the degree of force was reasonable in the circumstances.
- *Can you use force if force is expected to be used at some point in the future?* The threat must be immediate or at least imminent – as in, it must be expected in the very near future. If that danger has passed, then there is no necessity to use force.
- *Can you use force when you instigated or provoked the attack?* It depends. The defence is still available where the defendant provokes the violence. However, if that violence was provoked specifically in order to allow the defendant to attack the victim, then the defendant may not be able to rely on the defence. It would depend on whether the force used by the defendant was legitimately in defence of himself or not (eg in situations where the tables had turned on the defendant as the original instigator).

If the force used was not necessary, then the defence will fail. If it was necessary to use force, the next question will be whether it was reasonable in the circumstances as the defendant honestly believed them to be.

Reasonable force

What is considered **reasonable force** in the circumstances is a question of fact for the jury. The question is an objective one and permits the jury to take into account a number of factors, including the type and amount of force used.

Key term: reasonable force

Force is reasonable if it is regarded as being 'proportionate' in the circumstances. Disproportionate (or excessive) force, therefore, will not be reasonable.

In practicality, this is quite a straightforward question and the defendant is given a significant degree of latitude. We can break down the relevant principles relating to the use of reasonable force in the following manner:

- *On what basis is the defendant's response judged?* The defendant's response is judged in light of the circumstances as he honestly believed them to be. This is an objective test, though the defendant's beliefs are a relevant factor.
- *What does 'in the heat of the moment' mean?* The defendant's response must be judged in the knowledge that he may have had to act in the heat of the moment (ie where he has little time to consider how to respond). In this situation, the jury are required to take into account the fact that he may not have been able to weigh up precisely the amount of force needed to defend themselves or another.
- *Of what relevance is the defendant's belief that he used reasonable force?* If the defendant does no more than what they 'honestly and instinctively thought was necessary', that is strong, though not conclusive, evidence that only reasonable action was taken.
- *What other factors can be taken into account by the jury?* The jury are entitled to take any relevant information into account when deciding whether the force used was reasonable.

Whether the force used was reasonable therefore depends upon the threat the defendant is faced with. For example, shooting someone in the back while they are running away – as occurred in the infamous case *R v Martin (Anthony)* [2001] EWCA Crim 2245 – is clearly a disproportionate use of force (nor would it be necessary) (see **Practice example 4.3**).

Practice example 4.3

Karen is walking home from the shops late one evening when she sees a man walking towards her. She notices that he is holding something shiny that Karen thinks may be a knife. As the man approaches her, she strikes out with the bottle of wine she is holding in her hand, smashing it on the side of his head. The man suffers serious lacerations to his face. He was merely approaching Karen to ask her for directions and the shiny object in his hand was a pen.

Has Karen used reasonable force?

Karen has made a mistake about the need to use force and the question that must be asked is whether she used reasonable force in the circumstances as she honestly believed them to be. As she was alone at night and she thought that the man had a knife, her use of force may very well be found reasonable in the circumstances. Moreover, if she was acting honestly and instinctively, as appears to be the case here, this would suggest her use of force was reasonable.

Exam warning

Be aware that whether force is disproportionate will depend on the facts of any given case. Naturally, the greater degree of risk to D (as they believed the situation to be), the more force that may be used. If the danger posed to D has passed (in the sense that D was in danger, but is no longer), then the force is likely to be considered excessive. Look out for this kind of situation in an MCQ.

Mistake and reasonable force

If a mistake is made about the amount of force that it is reasonable to use in a given situation, this is a mistake as to law and is not a mistake upon which the defendant can rely. This is simply another way of restating that whether the force used is reasonable is an objective assessment for the jury.

Psychiatric conditions and reasonable force

While psychiatric conditions can be relevant to whether the force was necessary in the circumstances, they are irrelevant to the determination of whether the defendant's force was reasonable. If a defendant has been charged with murder, and is suffering, for example, from insane delusions, the appropriate defence would be diminished responsibility. Equally, a defendant may also allege a loss of self-control, which is similar to self-defence (see **Chapter 5**).

Summary: what do we know about self-defence?

In what circumstances can force be used?	Force can be used to defend yourself, others and property, and in the prevention of crime or the apprehension of offenders.
What amounts to a necessary use of force?	This is a subjective estimation. The question is whether it was necessary to use force in the circumstances as D believed them to be.
What amounts to reasonable force?	This is not a purely objective question as the amount of force used is viewed in the circumstances as D believed them to be. The question then is whether the amount of force was objectively reasonable in the circumstances as D believed them to be.

Householders and the use of force

The 'householder defence' was introduced to address concerns about the amount of force householders could use against those who trespass into a residence.

Exam warning

The householder defence is restricted to the use of self-defence (of oneself or others) – it cannot be used when D is acting in defence of property, to prevent crime or to effect or assist in the lawful arrest of offenders. Be aware of this when it comes to considering MCQs.

The statutory scheme for householders is laid out in s 76(8A) Criminal Justice and Immigration Act (CJIA) 2008. **Figure 4.6** (overleaf) outlines the elements of this defence.

We shall consider each element in turn.

The defendant must be a householder

This is a term undefined in the CJIA 2008. Given that the statute refers to 'householder' and not 'owner' or 'tenant', this provision is intended to benefit any person lawfully residing at the dwelling (whether permanently or temporarily). This understanding is furthered by the fact that the defendant must not be a trespasser at the time force is used. Thus, a burglar in a house could not then use force against another burglar and claim the defence.

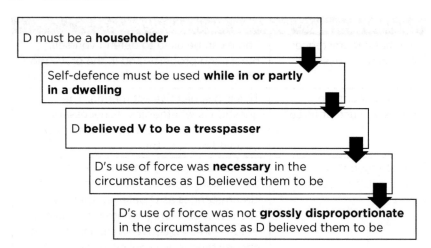

D must be a **householder**

Self-defence must be used **while in or partly in a dwelling**

D **believed V to be a tresspasser**

D's use of force was **necessary** in the circumstances as D believed them to be

D's use of force was not **grossly disproportionate** in the circumstances as D believed them to be

Figure 4.6: Elements of householder self-defence

Force must be used while in, or partly in, a dwelling

The force used must be while the defendant is:

- in a building, or part of a building, that is a dwelling or forces accommodation (or both); or
- partly in a building, or part of a building, that is a dwelling or forces accommodation (or both).

There are a number of features to this element, each of which can be considered in turn (see **Table 4.2**).

Table 4.2: Meaning of force used in a building

Element	Explanation
'a building, or part of a building, that is a dwelling'	Force must be used in, or partly in, a 'building', which must be a dwelling. A building is defined as including a vehicle or vessel (and thus the provision extends to individuals who live in caravans or houseboats), and forces accommodation.
	A 'dwelling' is not defined in the legislation but would simply refer to a place of residence.
'force used by D while in or partly in'	This provision protects householders who use force at the threshold of their home. For example, Mark uses force against Sam as she is climbing through a window, or is at the doorstep of the house. What is not made clear is where a 'building' stops. It is assumed that this is at the boundaries of the building itself and 'building' does not include the garden.

The definition at s 76(8A) extends to premises that have multiple uses, so where the living premises are joined and accessible, for example:

- A family who live above a shop or a pub, which is accessible from the dwelling, will benefit from the defence where an intruder has entered the shop or pub.
- A soldier living in forces accommodation may be living in one area and working in another and an intrusion into the working area will trigger the defence.

The defendant believes that the victim is a trespasser

It is not a question of whether the victim was a trespasser in civil law but whether the defendant *believed* that the victim was a trespasser. This then includes the following situations:

- where the defendant believes the victim to have *entered* a building as a trespasser
- where the defendant believes that the victim *is* in the building as a trespasser, whether or not he originally entered lawfully.

The defendant's belief is all that is important here. The belief need not be reasonable and may be mistaken (see **Practice example 4.4**).

Practice example 4.4

Jason goes into a cafe for a coffee. After drinking it, he realises he needs the toilet and asks the proprietor where the toilets are. The proprietor replies that they are out of order, but that Jason is welcome to use a private toilet that is in the cafe but serves a flat behind the building and directs him there. Jason uses the toilet and, as he opens the toilet door, he realises a young woman is standing outside. The young woman, Kylie, mistakes Jason for an intruder, screams and then slams the toilet door on to his hand, breaking three of Jason's fingers. Kylie lives in the flat adjoining the cafe.

Can Kylie claim the householder defence?

Kylie has encountered Jason believing him to be a trespasser and in part of the building that is adjoined to a dwelling. It does not matter that Jason may still technically be in the cafe, nor does it matter that he has the proprietor's permission to be on the premises. The real issue would be whether the force used by Kylie is reasonable.

Necessary to use force

This is the same test as applied in respect of non-householders (see **page 76, 'Force is necessary in the circumstances'**).

Reasonable force

In a householder case, the degree of force used will not be reasonable in the circumstances as the defendant believed them to be if it was 'grossly disproportionate' in those circumstances. In *R v Ray* [2017] EWCA Crim 1391, the Court of Appeal clarified that the jury had to consider two questions. These questions have been laid out in **Figure 4.7**.

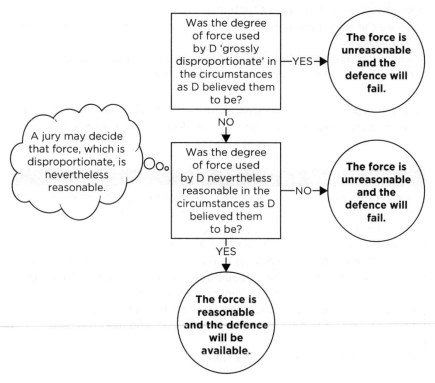

Figure 4.7: Determining whether force was grossly disproportionate

Although the force used by the defendant may be disproportionate it can still, in the circumstances, amount to reasonable force. This latitude then only extends to explaining to the jury that while grossly disproportionate force defeats the defence, anything less than that *may* be reasonable.

Exam warning

Be aware that while householders may use disproportionate force, and it still could be considered reasonable, if a non-householder uses force that is considered disproportionate, then it is not capable of being reasonable. An MCQ may seek to test your knowledge of this distinction (see **Practice example 4.5**).

Practice example 4.5

Jensen awoke to find a burglar in his home. He went downstairs and saw that the burglar was putting an urn containing his grandmother's ashes into a bag. The burglar saw Jensen and ran out of the house. Jensen chased him down the street, grabbed hold of him and dragged him into a nearby park. Once Jensen had restrained him, he then hit the burglar several times, intending to cause grievous bodily harm (GBH).

Can Jensen rely on the householder defence?

Although the burglar had initially entered a building as a trespasser, he had then departed, and Jensen cannot rely on the householder defence as he has not used force while in or partly in a building. Considering the ordinary principles of self-defence, while Jensen is seemingly defending his property, he is not under any immediate threat. The 'recovery' of stolen property is not a valid excuse to use force. Therefore, it is unnecessary to use force in these circumstances.

Revision tip

Keep the operation of proportionate force simple across both householders and non-householders:
- *Non-householders*: force is *only* reasonable if it is proportionate.
- *Householders*: force may be reasonable if it is not grossly disproportionate, even if it is disproportionate in the circumstances.

Summary: what do we know about the householder defence?	
Who amounts to a householder?	Any person who is lawfully residing in a dwelling (ie not a trespasser).
Who is a trespasser?	The focus is on whether D believed that the intruder was a trespasser.
Does a building just mean a house?	No, what amounts to a building is much broader than this and includes vehicles or vessels that are used as a dwelling and where an intruder has entered part of a building that is adjoined to a dwelling.
Can a householder use disproportionate force and claim the defence?	It depends whether that force is held to be reasonable in the circumstances. Where the force is grossly disproportionate, D will not be able to use the defence. Where lesser force is used, it will be a question for the finders of fact as to whether this amounts to reasonable force.

■ KEY POINT CHECKLIST

This chapter has covered the following key knowledge points. You can use these to structure your revision, ensuring you recall the key details for each point, as covered in this chapter.

• Intoxication is capable of acting as a defence to a criminal charge where the defendant, as a result of his intoxication, lacks the mens rea for the offence. Whether intoxication may operate as a defence varies according to whether the intoxication is voluntary or involuntary.

• Voluntary intoxication may act as a defence to specific-intent offences but not basic-intent offences. Involuntary intoxication may act as a defence to any crime, so long as the defendant lacks the mens rea for the offence.

• Self-defence will act as a defence where the defendant uses force in order to defend himself, another or his property.

• In order to rely on self-defence, there must first have been a necessity to use force on the facts as the defendant believes them to be. Second, the jury must be sure that the defendant's force is reasonable in the circumstances.

- Extra latitude is afforded to householders who use force in defence of themselves or another while in a dwelling. The amount of force used by the defendant must not be grossly disproportionate.

■ KEY TERMS AND CONCEPTS

- intoxication (**page 70**)
- specific intent (**page 72**)
- basic intent (**page 72**)
- dangerous drugs (**page 73**)
- non-dangerous drugs (**page 73**)
- reasonable force (**page 79**)

■ SQE1-STYLE QUESTIONS

QUESTION 1

A woman consumed a quantity of LSD and while hallucinating thought her boyfriend was a demon and killed him. She cannot remember the events and admits she voluntarily consumed the drug. She has been charged with manslaughter.

Will the woman be able to rely on the defence of intoxication?

A. Yes, as the woman has not formed the mens rea of a specific-intent offence due to her intoxication.

B. No, intoxication is only available where a person has consumed alcohol.

C. No, intoxication is only available as a defence where a person has become involuntarily intoxicated.

D. No, the woman has ingested a dangerous drug and has been charged with a basic-intent offence.

E. Yes, the woman consumed a non-dangerous drug and is then involuntarily intoxicated.

QUESTION 2

A man visits his friend's house and has a couple of drinks. He is told by his friend that they are low-alcohol drinks, but they are actually quite alcoholic (5.7 ABV). When the man leaves, he sees his ex-wife in the street, runs over to her and pushes her over intentionally. He now claims he would not ordinarily have done such a thing, but he was involuntarily intoxicated. The man is charged with a battery (intending or being reckless as to applying unlawful force).

Can the man rely on the defence of involuntary intoxication?

A. Yes, the man would not normally have acted this way and his inhibitions had been lowered by his involuntary intoxication.

B. Yes, involuntary intoxication supplies a defence where a person is not to blame for getting themselves into a state of intoxication.

C. No, the man's consumption of the drink does not amount to involuntary intoxication and the man formed the mens rea for the offence.

D. No, involuntary intoxication is not available where a person commits a basic-intent offence.

E. Yes, as the man was not reckless in his consumption of the drink.

QUESTION 3

A man had been drinking heavily at his local pub for several hours and was unsteady on his feet. Upon leaving the pub, he noticed a teenager walking towards him carrying a cricket bat. The teenager shouted, 'You alright mate?' The man misheard and thought the teenager had shouted 'You better run mate!' The man mistakenly thought he was about to be attacked and punched the teenager to the ground.

Can the man use the defence of self-defence?

A. Yes, the defence can be founded on a mistake as to the need to use self-defence.

B. No, a person cannot make a pre-emptive strike.

C. No, there was no immediacy to the threat.

D. Yes, the force used was reasonable in the circumstances as the man honestly (but mistakenly) believed them to be.

E. No, a person cannot rely on an intoxicated mistake as to the need to use self-defence.

QUESTION 4

A woman decided to play a trick on her friend and lay behind the bushes at the end of her friend's garden, waiting for him to come home from work. When her friend appeared, she burst out of the bushes intending to scare the man. The friend picked up a nearby shovel and hit the woman with it, killing her on impact. The man has been charged with murder and the trial judge has ruled the defence of self-defence is not available.

Is the trial judge correct to remove self-defence from the jury?

A. Yes, as it was merely a prank and it was unnecessary to use any force.

B. Yes, there is no defence of self-defence to murder.

C. No, the jury merely need to conclude that reasonable force was used.

D. No, the question of whether it was necessary to use force and whether that force was reasonable in those circumstances is one for the jury.

E. Yes, self-defence is unavailable to specific-intent offences.

QUESTION 5

A woman was at home one evening when she heard someone come into her home. She ran into the kitchen and picked up a knife. She then confronted the shadowy figure and stabbed him several times. When she switched on the kitchen light, she realised the 'intruder' was her friend who she had asked to come around to drop off her spare keys. The judge directed the jury that they should find she acted in self-defence unless the force she used was grossly disproportionate.

Is the judge correct in his direction to the jury?

A. Yes, the householder defence means any force short of that which is grossly disproportionate force amounts to reasonable force.

B. No, force that is disproportionate is reasonable, but grossly disproportionate force is not.

C. Yes, the judge can phrase this to the jury in any way he deems appropriate.

D. No, the jury should be directed that if the force used is grossly disproportionate the defence will fail, if it was not, the jury should ask itself whether the force used was reasonable.

E. No, the jury should be directed to consider whether the force used was disproportionate, if it was the defence will fail.

■ ANSWERS TO QUESTIONS

Answers to 'What do you know already?' questions at the start of the chapter

1) A general defence is one that is capable of applying to all offences (eg self-defence), while a special defence only applies to a limited number of offences (eg diminished responsibility is only a defence to murder). A complete defence is one that rids the defendant of criminal liability (eg self-defence), whereas a partial defence is one that reduces the defendant's liability to a lesser offence (eg intoxication may reduce s 18 GBH with intent to s 20 GBH).

2) A basic-intent offence is understood as being one where the offence is capable of being committed recklessly (eg common assault). A specific-intent offence is one where the offence is primarily committed intentionally (eg murder), or where the mens rea is ulterior to the actus reus.

3) In order to rely on self-defence, the defendant's force must be 'proportionate' in the circumstances, meaning that the defendant has used reasonable force in defence of himself or another. Excessive force will not be proportionate or reasonable.

4) False. A defendant cannot rely on a mistaken belief as to whether force was necessary in the circumstances if that belief was induced by voluntary intoxication.

Answers to end-of-chapter SQE1-style questions

Question 1:
   The correct answer was D. This is because the woman would be subject to the rules governing voluntary intoxication as she has taken a dangerous drug and had been charged with a basic-intent offence. Manslaughter is a basic-intent offence, so option A is wrong. Option B is incorrect on account that the rules of intoxication apply equally to drugs or alcohol. Option C is wrong because it ignores the rules relating to voluntary intoxication and option E is wrong on account that LSD is a dangerous drug.

Question 2:
   The correct answer was C. This is because the man knew he was drinking alcohol, and it is irrelevant whether he was aware of the strength of the alcohol or not, so this cannot amount to involuntary intoxication and he also formed the mens rea for the offence. Option

A is incorrect on account that a drunken intent is still an intent and lowered inhibitions is no defence. Option B ignores the fact that the man still formed the mens rea and thus is wrong. Option D is wrong because involuntary intoxication is capable of being used for all offences, and in any event the man is not involuntarily intoxicated. Recklessness as to consumption is only relevant where the drug is a non-dangerous one, for which alcohol is not (so option E is wrong).

Question 3:

The correct answer was E. Where a mistake is made about the need to use force because of voluntary intoxication, no defence of self-defence is available to either a basic- or specific-intent offence. Option A is incorrect on account that while a mistake can found a defence of self-defence, a mistake induced by intoxication cannot. Option B is wrong as pre-emptive strikes can be relied on to use force. Option C is incorrect on account that the man is to be judged on the facts as he believed them to be (and the man believed he was about to be attacked with a cricket bat). Option D ignores the fact that the man was intoxicated and the fact that a mistake cannot be made as to how much force is reasonable.

Question 4:

The correct answer was D. This is because the question of whether it was necessary to use force is one for the jury, which must take into account the man's honest belief. They may take into account how reasonable it is that he held that belief, but he is not automatically deprived of the defence as the use of force was, as here, unnecessary. Option A ignores the fact that the necessity to use force must be judged on the facts as the man believed them to be (the man would not know that this was a prank). Option B is wrong as self-defence can be a defence to murder. Option C is wrong as it ignores the first stage of the test for self-defence: whether force was necessary in the circumstances. Option E is not sufficiently precise as to why self-defence is a valid defence and thus cannot be the best answer.

Question 5:

The correct answer was D. This is because the correct direction asks first whether the force used was grossly disproportionate. If so, the defence fails. If it was not, the jury should then ask itself whether the force used was reasonable. Disproportionate force may be reasonable, but this is a question for the jury. Option A is incorrect because it ignores the second question to be asked by the jury: whether the force was nevertheless reasonable in the circumstances. Option B misstates the law: disproportionate force is not automatically reasonable, it depends on the assessment of the jury. Option C is wrong because it ignores the directions laid down by the courts as to the two questions the jury must ask. Option E ignores the fact that disproportionate force may be considered reasonable in the circumstances.

■ KEY CASES, RULES, STATUTES AND INSTRUMENTS

The SQE1 Assessment Specification does not require you to know any case names, or statutory materials, for the topic of general defences.

5

Homicide offences

■ MAKE SURE YOU KNOW

This chapter will cover the homicide offences of murder, voluntary manslaughter and involuntary manslaughter. For the SQE1 assessment, you are required to know the law relating to murder, the partial defences of diminished responsibility and loss of control, and the offences of unlawful act manslaughter and gross negligence manslaughter. You are required to know each offence/defence and be able to apply the legal principles and rules appropriately and effectively to realistic client-based and ethical problems and situations for your SQE1 assessment.

The SQE1 Assessment Specification has not identified that candidates are required to recall/recite any case names, or statutory materials, for the topic of homicide.

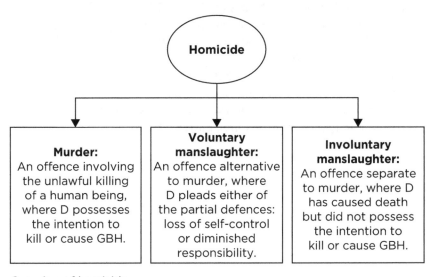

Overview of homicide

■ SQE ASSESSMENT ADVICE

As you work through this chapter, remember to pay particular attention in your revision to:
• the actus reus and mens rea of the offence of murder
• the defence of loss of control
• the defence of diminished responsibility
• the elements that must be proven to establish unlawful act manslaughter
• the elements that must be proven to establish gross negligence manslaughter.

■ WHAT DO YOU KNOW ALREADY?

Have a go at these questions before reading this chapter. If you find some difficult or cannot remember the answers, make a note to look more closely at that area during your revision.

1) Fill in the blank: the mens rea for murder is _____.

   [Murder, pages 95–98]

2) True or false: the defence of loss of control requires an actual loss of self-control.

   [Loss of control, pages 99–104]

3) True or false: the burden of proof for diminished responsibility is on the prosecution to disprove the defence.

   [Diminished responsibility, pages 104–108]

4) To be liable for the offence of unlawful act manslaughter, is the defendant required to foresee a risk of death, or at least a risk of serious bodily harm?

   [Unlawful act manslaughter, pages 108–112]

5) How might a judge direct the jury on what amounts to 'gross negligence' for the offence of gross negligence manslaughter?

   [Gross negligence manslaughter, pages 112–116]

INTRODUCTION TO HOMICIDE OFFENCES

'Homicide' is an umbrella term used to describe a set of offences in which the death of another has been brought about by the defendant. In that regard, they all share a common actus reus. There are, however, significant differences between them, and you need to pay careful attention to the mens rea of an offence and whether the defendant has a partial defence in seeking to distinguish between them.

Table 5.1 provides a summary of these homicide offences.

Table 5.1: Homicide offences summary

Offence	Summary
Murder	The unlawful killing of a human being under the King's peace with malice aforethought.
Voluntary manslaughter (loss of control)	D has intentionally killed or has killed with an intention to do serious harm but had experienced a loss of control. This has arisen from a qualifying trigger and a reasonable person would have acted in the same, or a similar, way as D.
Voluntary manslaughter (diminished responsibility)	D has intentionally killed or killed with an intention to do serious harm but had experienced an abnormality of mental functioning arising from a recognised medical condition. This abnormality had substantially impaired their ability to understand the nature of their conduct, form a rational judgment or exercise self-control and provides an explanation for the killing.
Involuntary manslaughter (unlawful act manslaughter)	D commits a criminal act (not an omission) that is objectively dangerous and causes the death of the victim.
Involuntary manslaughter (gross negligence manslaughter)	A killing where D owes a duty of care to the victim, that duty has been breached in a manner that poses a risk of death and D's act or omission in bringing about that death can be characterised as grossly negligent.

MURDER

The most serious homicide-related offence is **murder**, which is a common-law offence.

Key term: murder

Murder is the unlawful killing of a human being under the King's peace with malice aforethought.

The offence of murder can therefore be broken down into the five elements outlined in **Figure 5.1**.

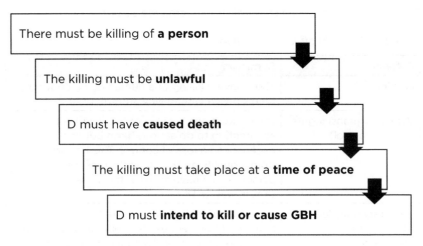

Figure 5.1: Elements of murder

Killing of a person

The killing of 'a person' merely requires that the victim is a human being (see **Practice example 5.1**).

Practice example 5.1

Tariq stabbed Bushra in the abdomen during an argument. Unbeknown to Tariq, Bushra was four months pregnant and as a result of the stabbing the foetus was killed.

Has Tariq committed the offence of murder?

In law, a foetus is not a person and though there are specific offences that could be charged in respect of the killing of an unborn child, the foetus is only recognised as a person when they have been born alive. Therefore, Tariq cannot be guilty of murder.

You must then be born to amount to a human being, and this includes where a child is born but requires continuing medical assistance to survive.

Killing must be unlawful

An 'unlawful' killing requires all elements of the actus reus and mens rea for murder to be fulfilled and that there are no available defences, such as self-defence (considered in **Chapter 4**).

Exam warning

Please remember that not all defences are available if a defendant is charged with murder. For example, consent cannot be given by a victim to their own killing. Consent is considered in **Chapter 6** in respect of non-fatal offences.

Defendant must have caused death

Murder is a result crime (see **Chapter 1**); this means that the prosecution must prove that the defendant was both the factual and legal cause of death. As every individual will die eventually, we are looking for an *acceleration* of death. In law, a person is considered as having died when they are brain dead.

Killing must take place at a time of peace

Reference to 'the King's peace' simply excludes the killing of enemy forces during a time of war.

Intention to kill or cause grievous bodily harm

The mens rea of murder is that the defendant must kill with **malice aforethought**.

Key term: malice aforethought

'Malice aforethought' is a technical term and there is no requirement for premeditation or ill will. The defendant need only intend to kill or intend to cause grievous bodily harm (GBH – discussed in **Chapter 6**, essentially means 'serious harm').

Intention was discussed in **Chapter 1** and the mens rea for murder features alternative intentions. **Table 5.2** identifies these alternatives.

Table 5.2: Intention for murder

Intention variation	Explanation and examples
Direct intention to kill	D possesses the intention to bring about another person's death. For example, Mark stands directly in front of Sam and shoots her in the head with a gun. Mark clearly has the intention to kill.
Direct intention to cause GBH	D does not possess the intention to kill, but does possess the intention to cause serious injury to another person. For example, Sam punches Mark in the face numerous times; Mark dies from his injuries. Sam did not intend to kill Mark, but did intend to cause him serious harm.
Oblique intention to kill	D does not possess the intention to kill, but death was a virtual certainty as a result of D's conduct, and D appreciated this certainty. For example, Mark shoots Sam in the stomach with a gun. Mark does not wish to kill Sam, but he does appreciate that death is a virtually certain result of shooting someone in the stomach.
Oblique intention to cause GBH	D does not possess the intention to cause GBH, but serious injury was a virtual certainty as a result of D's conduct, and D appreciated this certainty. Sam throws a number of large rocks from her bedroom window at Mark, who is standing outside on the ground. Sam intends to throw the rocks at Mark's head but does not wish to cause Mark serious injury. Sam appreciates, however, that serious injury is a virtually certain result of throwing large rocks at another person from a great height.

Summary: what do we know about murder?	
What is the meaning of 'unlawful killing'?	Murder requires that D accelerate the death of another person. This is simply a test of causation. Death occurs when an individual is brain dead.
Who is a 'person' for the purposes of murder?	A person, or 'human being', is someone who has been born alive.
What does 'under the King's peace' mean?	Murder is only committed where the death is caused during a time of peace (ie not a time of war).
What is the mens rea for murder?	D must either intend to kill or intend to cause serious harm. D's intention may be direct or oblique.

INTRODUCING VOLUNTARY MANSLAUGHTER

There are three partial defences to the offence of murder: loss of control, diminished responsibility and suicide pact. Suicide pact is not an examinable topic on SQE1. If any of these defences are made out, the defendant will be liable for the offence of voluntary manslaughter, opening up the possibility of a lesser sentence than the mandatory life sentence imposed for murder.

Revision tip

Do not be confused by the terminology in respect of voluntary manslaughter. Think about it this way: voluntary manslaughter is an *offence*. A defendant can be convicted of this offence if he successfully pleads one of the partial *defences*. Loss of self-control and diminished responsibility are both *defences* to a charge of murder.

LOSS OF CONTROL

The defence of loss of control is defined at s 54(1) Coroners and Justice Act (CJA) 2009 and can be broken down into three elements (see **Figure 5.2**).

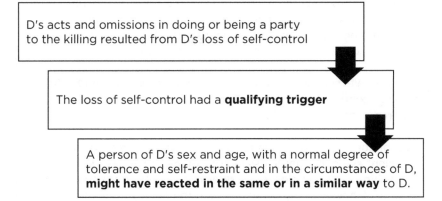

D's acts and omissions in doing or being a party to the killing resulted from D's loss of self-control

The loss of self-control had a **qualifying trigger**

A person of D's sex and age, with a normal degree of tolerance and self-restraint and in the circumstances of D, **might have reacted in the same or in a similar way** to D.

Figure 5.2: Elements of loss of control

All three elements of the defence must be satisfied for the defence to be successful. We will consider each element in turn.

The defendant loses his self-control

For the defence to be left to the jury, there must first be a **loss of self-control**.

Key term: loss of self-control

A loss of control is understood to amount to more than irritation or even serious anger, it requires that the defendant has lost their ability to reason clearly.

While a loss of control will often be sudden, s 54(2) clarifies that suddenness is not an element of the defence. This allows for the situations where the defendant's reaction has built up over a period of time, for example where there has been a history of domestic abuse between the defendant and the victim.

While the loss of control need not be sudden, it must be actual, in that the defendant must have suffered a 'loss of the ability to act in accordance with considered judgment or a loss of the normal powers of reasoning' (*R v Jewell* [2014] EWCA Crim 414) (see **Practice example 5.2**).

Practice example 5.2

Jenny has suffered domestic abuse at the hands of her partner, Terri, for three years. One evening, Terri attacks Jenny with a knife and Jenny escapes, runs up the stairs and locks herself in their bedroom. Fifteen minutes later Jenny creeps down the stairs to find Terri sitting in the kitchen with her head on the table. Jenny does not know whether Terri is asleep and, fearing another attack, she hits her on the head with a heavy vase. Terri dies immediately.

Jenny admits she intended serious injury but claims she had suffered a loss of control resulting from Terri's initial attack. Has Jenny suffered a loss of control?

Loss of control is a question for the jury if the judge finds there is sufficient evidence that a loss of control may have been suffered. In reaching their decision a jury does not have to find a *sudden* loss of control, however any delay between the qualifying trigger and the reaction (the killing) can be taken into account. If the defendant has had the opportunity to calm down, she may have regained her control.

A further caveat to this is where the defendant acts 'in a considered desire for revenge'. Ensuring retaliatory killings do not benefit from the defence is valuable. This does provide, however, a further hurdle for battered spouses to rely on the defence where there is a delay between the trigger and the killing.

Revision tip

Make sure that you have a look at the explanatory notes to the CJA 2009. They are useful for revision and provide examples of how the defence operates in practice.

Qualifying triggers

The next element for the defence to be made out is that the source of the loss of control must fall within one of the 'qualifying triggers'. Either trigger can be satisfied, or the defence may rely on a combination of the two triggers.

Fear trigger

This trigger is satisfied if the defendant loses self-control because they were in fear of serious violence being used against themselves, or against another identified person, by the victim. This is a subjective test, with the focus on:

• whether the defendant *actually feared* the use of violence
• whether what they feared was *serious* violence.

There is no definition of 'serious violence' in the CJA 2009, but it can be assumed to equate to injuries that we would define as GBH (eg broken bones, serious concussion and substantial blood loss).

Anger trigger

This trigger is satisfied if the defendant loses their self-control because they had:

• responded to something 'said or done'
• what was said or done was of an 'extremely grave character'
• what was said or done had caused the defendant 'to have a justifiable sense of being seriously wronged'.

How these terms are construed is not detailed in the CJA 2009 but have been considered by the courts (see **Table 5.3** overleaf).

Both triggers are subject to limitations, as detailed below.

Limitations on the triggers

• If fear or anger is incited by the defendant then the trigger may not be satisfied. This is limited to where the defendant has purposefully manipulated the victim into acting.

Table 5.3: Understanding the anger trigger

Terminology	Objective or subjective	Explanation and examples
extremely grave character	Objective	Circumstances that would not constitute those of an 'extremely grave character' include minor aggravations (a crying baby, a badly parked car, poor customer service) or where the gravity of it flows from a personal bias (eg a daughter telling her homophobic parent that she is gay).
justifiable sense	Objective	Justifiable simply means that a reasonable person would feel similarly wronged in the circumstances of the defendant. For example, an intruder into a home may feel seriously wronged if the homeowner threatened him and told him to leave, but this would not be justifiable in the circumstances.
of being seriously wronged	Subjective	D must personally feel seriously wronged. Note that, as per the above, if D claims to be seriously wronged, but this is not objectively justifiable in the circumstances, the trigger cannot be satisfied.

- Equally, if the defendant has incited the thing to be done or said for the purpose of providing an excuse to use violence, then the defendant cannot claim to have a *justifiable* sense of being seriously wronged.
- The final limitation has been the most problematic. Sexual infidelity cannot be the thing 'done or said'. On the face of it, this would mean a confession of infidelity or being caught in the act of infidelity could never engage the trigger. In *R v Clinton, R v Parker, R v Evans* [2012] EWCA Crim 2, the defendant had killed his wife after she had confessed to infidelity with a number of men and had also taunted him about his failed attempts at suicide. At trial, the trial judge had withdrawn the loss of control defence from the jury on the ground it was excluded. The Court of Appeal allowed the appeal and made the following clarifications:
  - Where sexual infidelity is the *sole thing said or done* it is to be disregarded.

- Where sexual infidelity is an *essential part* of the context in which the loss of control occurred it is not to be excluded in a determination of whether other things 'said and done' were grave enough to amount to the trigger (see **Practice example 5.3**).
- Sexual infidelity is not excluded from the objective test at 54(1)(c).

Practice example 5.3

Sally has returned home to find her husband having consensual sex with her sister. Her husband responds by shouting at Sally and making clear – using aggressive and hurtful language – that she has prompted his infidelity. Sally snaps and kills her husband. She is seeking to rely on the loss of control defence to partially excuse her actions.

Is she barred from relying on the trigger by s 55(4) because the things said and done related to her husband's sexual infidelity?

No, Sally would still be able to rely on the defence (subject to all the necessary elements being made out). Where sexual infidelity is integral to and forms an essential part of the context in which to make a just evaluation of whether a qualifying trigger properly falls within the ambit of s 55(3) and (4), the prohibition does not operate to exclude it.

Reasonable person test
The final limb of the test is stated in s 54(1)(c) and requires that:
- a person of the defendant's sex and age
- with a normal degree of tolerance and self-restraint
- and in the circumstances of the defendant
- might have reacted in the same or in a similar way to the defendant.

This is a reasonable person test – an objective yardstick against which all defendants must be judged – to ensure the killing was justifiable. Sex and age are standard characteristics attributed under such a test and may be of particular relevance if the defendant is young.

The defendant is expected to be able to exercise the same standard of tolerance and self-restraint as an average member of society. Though the test speaks of 'the circumstances' of the defendant, this test of steadfastness cannot be altered to take account of a defendant's particular vulnerabilities (ie his general capacity for tolerance or self-restraint).

Being intoxicated is not a relevant circumstance when it only impacts upon a defendant's ability to control himself, however if the defendant were taunted about an existing alcohol addiction (amounting to a qualifying trigger) this would likely form part of the circumstances for consideration here. Likewise, the battered spouse who killed their abuser would have their background of domestic abuse taken into account.

Summary: what do we know about loss of self-control?	
When will a killing result from a loss of control?	It must be proven that D actually lost his self-control and that the killing was not caused by some other reasons, eg a considered desire for revenge. The loss of control need not be sudden.
What are the 'qualifying triggers'?	The loss of self-control must be attributed to either a fear of serious violence from the victim to D or another person, a thing said or done that constituted circumstances of an extremely grave character and caused D to have a justifiable sense of being seriously wronged, or a combination of both. There are certain exclusions to the operation of these triggers.
What does it mean to say that another person 'might have reacted in the same or a similar way'?	A person of the same sex and age as D, with a normal degree of tolerance and self-restraint and in the circumstances of D, might have reacted in the same or a similar way. This is an objective test and is a question of fact for the jury.

DIMINISHED RESPONSIBILITY

The second partial defence to murder is that of **diminished responsibility**, found in s 2 of the Homicide Act (HA) 1957 (as amended by s 52 CJA 2009).

Key term: diminished responsibility
Diminished responsibility is *essentially* a defence of partial insanity, providing a justification for D, who is suffering from an abnormality of the mind but not a total loss of control.

As discussed in **Chapter 4**, diminished responsibility imposes a reverse legal burden, requiring the defendant to prove the existence of the defence to the civil standard (on the balance of probabilities).

The four elements that the defendant must establish to succeed in pleading the defence are broken down in **Figure 5.3**.

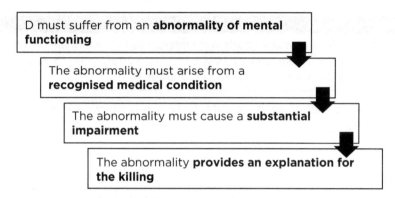

Figure 5.3: Elements of diminished responsibility

We will consider each element in turn.

Abnormality of mental functioning
An abnormality of mental functioning merely means that the defendant's mental functioning is abnormal, in that it departs from that of the ordinary, reasonable person (*R v Byrne* [1960] 2 QB 396).

Arising from a recognised medical condition
The defendant will need to provide psychiatric evidence that they are (or were) suffering from a recognised medical condition. 'Medical' is a broad term that encompasses mental conditions (eg schizophrenia and depression) and physical conditions (eg sleepwalking and diabetes). Ultimately, whether this amounts to a medical condition for the purpose of the defence and whether that has caused an abnormality of mental functioning is a question of fact for a jury.

Examples of recognised medical conditions in case law include:
• battered spouse syndrome
• psychopathic personality disorder
• depression.

Substantial impairment

The abnormality arising from the disorder must 'substantially impair' the defendant's ability to do one or more of the things detailed in s 2(1A) below. 'Substantial' should not usually require elaboration but, where it does, a jury should be directed that substantial is being used in the sense of a 'substantial meal' or a 'substantial salary'; it does not mean a more than trivial impairment (*R v Golds* [2016] UKSC 61).

Exam warning

Do not confuse how the courts have interpreted 'substantial' for the purposes of this defence with how it has been interpreted for the principle of causation considered in **Chapter 1**.

The abilities that must be substantially impaired are summarised in **Table 5.4**.

Table 5.4: Abilities that are substantially impaired

The abilities that must be impaired	Explanation and examples
'to understand the nature of D's conduct'	This is similar to the test for insanity but requires only a substantial impairment. For example, a person who kills without understanding the finality of that act (ie that an individual is dead) would satisfy this limb.
'to form a rational judgment'	An inability to act rationally may arise if an individual has suffered years of abuse and decides this is the only way to escape. Or, for example, where a husband kills his infirm wife as he can no longer care for her and does not believe she will be effectively cared for elsewhere.
'to exercise self-control'	An abnormality may limit an individual's ability to use self-restraint. For example, a serious brain injury or a psychiatric condition (eg battered spouse syndrome) could lead to an inability to control one's temper. This provides an alternative for individuals who fail to satisfy the objective limb of the loss of control defence because they cannot exercise a 'normal degree of tolerance and self-restraint'.

Explanation for the killing

The final element requires a causal link between the abnormality and the killing. Specifically, the abnormality of mental functioning must cause, or be a significant contributory factor in causing, the defendant to carry out that conduct. This is to ensure that the killing can be properly attributed to the impact of the abnormality and is not a matter of mere coincidence.

Additional points on diminished responsibility

Some final questions on diminished responsibility are dealt with in **Table 5.5**. Consider whether you know the answer to the question first, and then see the answer provided.

Table 5.5: Additional questions on diminished responsibility

Question	Answer
Can voluntary intoxication, arising from alcoholism, amount to a recognised medical condition?	Intoxication (by drink or drugs) cannot amount to a recognised medical condition. However, alcohol dependency syndrome, or brain damage arising from the same, can amount to a recognised medical condition and the jury can take account of the condition and any resultant intoxication.
Where D triggers a pre-existing condition such as schizophrenia because they have taken drink or drugs, can they rely on diminished responsibility?	Yes, if they still satisfy the elements of the defence. The jury can consider the psychiatric condition and, if the intoxication was a result of alcohol dependency, this can, as set out above, also be taken into consideration.
Where there is uncontroversial and uncontested medical/psychiatric evidence that D satisfied the defence, can a jury still reject the evidence and convict D of murder?	In such circumstances the judge should withdraw murder from the jury.

Summary: what do we know about diminished responsibility?	
What is an 'abnormality of mental functioning'?	Abnormality of mental functioning is understood as being a state of mind so different from that of ordinary human beings that the reasonable man would term it abnormal.
What is the meaning of a 'recognised medical condition'?	Medical evidence must be capable of discharging the burden on the accused to show, on the balance of probabilities, that each ingredient of the defence is made out.
What do we mean by 'substantial impairment'?	The abnormality must impair D's ability to (a) understand the nature of his own conduct, (b) form a rational judgment or (c) exercise self-control.
What is the requirement that the abnormality of mental functioning provides an 'explanation' for the killing?	There must be some causal link between D's abnormality of mental functioning and the killing.

INTRODUCING INVOLUNTARY MANSLAUGHTER

Where the defendant does not intend to kill or to cause serious injury, but has brought about the death of another, the relevant offences are to be found under the umbrella of 'involuntary manslaughter'. You are required to know two involuntary manslaughter offences for SQE1. These are:
• unlawful act manslaughter
• gross negligence manslaughter.

UNLAWFUL ACT MANSLAUGHTER

The first offence to consider is that of **unlawful act manslaughter**.

Key term: unlawful act manslaughter
Sometimes referred to as 'constructive manslaughter', this offence constructs liability for manslaughter from the commission of a criminal offence in circumstances where D did not possess the intention to kill or cause serious harm.

The elements of the offence are identified in **Figure 5.4** (*DPP v Newbury* [1977] AC 500).

We will consider each element in turn.

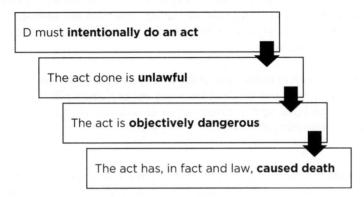

D must **intentionally do an act**

The act done is **unlawful**

The act is **objectively dangerous**

The act has, in fact and law, **caused death**

Figure 5.4: Elements of unlawful act manslaughter

Intentional act

The defendant must have:

- performed a positive act – an omission cannot form the basis of the offence. If death has resulted from a failure to act, and there was no intention to kill, the appropriate offence will be gross negligence manslaughter.
- acted deliberately (ie voluntarily).

Act is unlawful

'Unlawful' here simply means a criminal offence – a civil wrong cannot amount to an unlawful act. Nor will an offence that is satisfied by proof of negligence or a strict liability offence.

The unlawful act need not be a violent offence, any criminal offence (subject to the constraints above) will suffice. For example, unlawful act manslaughter has been constructed from:

- criminal damage
- burglary
- robbery.

The criminal offence must be proven in full. That is, the actus reus and the mens rea of the offence must be satisfied and there must not be an effective defence (see **Practice example 5.4**).

Practice example 5.4

James and Teddy, two teenage boys, are playing with a gun when James points the gun at Teddy and pulls the trigger, shooting his friend. Neither boy had expected the gun to fire a bullet as they had checked the chamber and seen no bullets. They had not realised that, when the trigger was pulled, the chamber would rotate and a bullet would be fired.

James has been charged with unlawful act manslaughter and the trial judge directs the jury that the mere act of pointing the gun at his friend and pulling the trigger amounts to an unlawful act. Has the judge directed the jury correctly as to what constitutes an unlawful act?

These are the facts of _R v Lamb_ [1967] 2 QB 981. It was held that the trial judge had erred in directing the jury as the relevant unlawful act must be identified and that this would be – on the facts – an assault. For an assault to be committed the victim must apprehend the application of immediate unlawful force. There was no such apprehension in _Lamb_ as neither boy expected a bullet would be fired. Moreover, there was no mens rea as there was no intention to cause such apprehension or apply force, nor was there subjective recklessness.

There is no requirement that the unlawful act is directed at the victim. For example, in _DPP v Newbury_, two boys pushed a concrete block on to a train. Their intention was merely to hit the train and the victim (the conductor) was killed when the block went through the train cab. Despite this, the boys remained liable for an offence.

That is objectively dangerous

The test for **dangerousness** is an objective test. It does not require any appreciation by the defendant that his act is dangerous: if the reasonable person sees an obvious risk of harm, the test will be satisfied.

Key term: dangerousness

The unlawful act must be such that all sober and reasonable people would inevitably recognise that it must subject the other person to, at least, the risk of some harm resulting therefrom, albeit not serious harm.

The reasonable person (who is always sober) must see an inevitable risk of some harm. There are a number of important points that flow from this test:

- 'Inevitable' narrows this test to where the risk is almost certain, foreseeing a risk as probable is not sufficient.
- The reasonable person need only foresee that *some* harm will result – there is no requirement for the reasonable man to foresee death or serious harm.
- The harm that is foreseen will normally be physical harm. No case has addressed whether the harm foreseen includes psychological harm, but it is likely this is now within the definition of harm (see **Chapter 6**).
- There is no requirement that the reasonable person foresees the particular form of harm (ie a wound) that results.
- The harm risked must be harm to the victim, this is 'the other person'.

Case law has clarified what knowledge can be given to the reasonable person in making this assessment of dangerousness (see **Table 5.6**).

Table 5.6: Knowledge of the reasonable person

Principle	Explanation and examples
Anything the reasonable person would have gleaned watching the events unfold.	In *R v Dawson* (1985) 81 Cr App R 150 it was confirmed that the objective test is undertaken upon the basis of the knowledge gained by the sober and reasonable man as though he were present at the scene and watched the events unfold.
	In *R v Watson* [1989] 2 All ER 865 a burglar verbally abused the elderly owner of the house he had broken into. It was held that it would have become obvious to the reasonable bystander during the course of the intrusion that the householder was elderly and frail.
The same knowledge D had at the time of the offence, including any preparations D has made.	D may have some special knowledge and this will be given to the reasonable person. For example, he may know D has a weak heart.
The reasonable man does not make unreasonable mistakes.	In *R v Ball* [1989] Crim LR 730 D had loaded a shotgun with cartridges from his pocket where he knew he had put a mix of live and blank rounds. He fired his gun at the victim claiming he had intended to frighten and had mistakenly thought he had loaded the gun with blanks. On appeal the Court of Appeal rejected his argument that an assessment of dangerousness should be based on a mistaken belief.

That causes death

The unlawful act must cause death in fact and law. This then involves an application of causation principles discussed in **Chapter 1.**

Summary: what do we know about unlawful act manslaughter?	
What do we mean by the requirement of an 'intentional act'?	D must perform an act (and not an omission) and must do so deliberately.
What does it mean to say that the act must be 'unlawful'?	The act performed by D must be a criminal offence; civil wrongs are insufficient. Likewise, offences that can be satisfied by mere negligence or are strict liability offences cannot form the basis for unlawful act manslaughter.
What is the meaning of an 'objectively dangerous' act?	The unlawful act must be one all sober and reasonable people would recognise as subjecting the other person to the risk of some harm resulting therefrom, albeit not serious harm.
The unlawful act must cause death. What does this mean?	The unlawful act must have accelerated the death of the victim, in that D is considered to be both the factual and legal cause of death.

GROSS NEGLIGENCE MANSLAUGHTER

Gross negligence manslaughter is the appropriate offence where:
• there is no unlawful act, or
• the death arises from an omission to act.

Key term: gross negligence manslaughter
This offence is unusual as it imparts liability for a serious criminal offence where D may not have consciously risked harm. Instead the offence is focused upon the conduct of D, which causes death, and whether this conduct can be characterised as grossly negligent (and thus justifying criminal punishment).

These elements of this offence were approved in *R v Adomako* [1995] 1 AC 171 and are set out in **Figure 5.5.**

We will consider each element in turn.

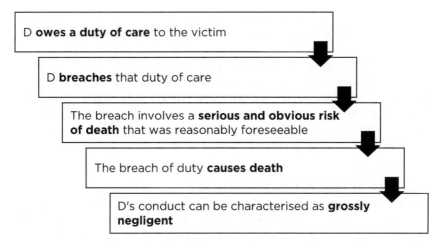

Figure 5.5: Elements of gross negligence manslaughter

The defendant owes a duty of care to the victim

The first requirement is that the defendant owes the victim a duty of care. Whether a duty exists will largely depend on the relationship between the parties. For example, a duty may exist between:

- a doctor to their patient
- an electrician and a householder who uses the services of the electrician
- a landlord and their tenant, who relies on the landlord's services.

The manner of approaching this element varies depending on whether the defendant is alleged to have committed an act or an omission.

Positive acts and the duty of care

If the death has resulted from a positive act, the court will simply use the ordinary principles of negligence to determine whether a duty is owed; in short, a defendant owes a duty to those who may suffer harm as a result of his actions. The criminal law is not constrained by any other tort principles that restrict where a duty would be found; for example, where the defendant and the victim are involved in a criminal enterprise a duty may still be found in the criminal law.

Omissions and the duty of care

Where death has resulted from a failure to act, it is necessary to first establish a duty to act. If you are satisfied that a duty to act exists, you would then consider whether there is an additional duty of care. The recognised duties to act have been discussed in **Chapter 1** and you will recall they are restricted to a number of narrow categories. In practicality, where there is a duty to act, there will also be a duty of care.

Who determines whether a duty of care exists?

Whether a duty of care exists is a matter of law, and thus a question for the judge. The jury will be instructed that a duty exists where this is indisputable (eg the case concerns a doctor/patient relationship). Where a duty of care may exist, the jury will be directed to consider whether the facts support the existence of that duty.

The duty of care has been breached

This test is objective and asks the jury to assess whether the defendant's conduct has fallen short of what would be expected of a reasonable person in that circumstance. Any special skills the defendant has will be given to the reasonable person in making that determination.

The breach involves a serious and obvious risk of death

In addition, the breach must be such that a reasonable person would foresee it would give rise to a serious and obvious risk of death. The state of knowledge at the time of the breach will be imputed to the reasonable person in making this estimation and is often key to whether there is an actionable breach in medical cases. An obvious risk is one that is present, clear and unambiguous. It is immediately apparent, rather than something that might become apparent on further investigation (see **Practice example 5.5**).

Practice example 5.5

Sally called her GP one Friday afternoon as she was concerned about her son, Billy. Billy had been suffering a range of symptoms, none of which were serious. Sally's GP suggested that, if Billy had not improved, they should come into the surgery on Monday morning. Billy died the next day. It was later established that Billy had died from a very rare disease.

Has the GP breached their duty of care?

This example is based on the facts of *R v Rudling* [2016] EWCA Crim 741. Here, the Court of Appeal reiterated that the risk of death must be obvious to a reasonable person with the same skills as D. This was a disease that no GP would have recognised and could not provide the basis for the offence of gross negligence manslaughter.

The breach has caused the death

Once again, the normal principles of causation must be satisfied.

The breach of duty was 'grossly negligent'

The breach of duty must be so bad that it is capable of being characterised by the jury as 'gross'. In *Adomako*, the House of Lords established that the jury should be asked to consider whether, 'having regard to the risk of death involved, was the conduct of the defendant so bad in all the circumstances as to amount to a criminal act or omission?'

Over the years there have been numerous attempts to define the concept of **gross negligence**. Some of these are detailed in **Figure 5.6**.

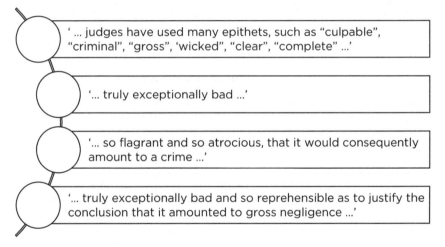

' ... judges have used many epithets, such as "culpable", "criminal", "gross", 'wicked", "clear", "complete" ...'

'... truly exceptionally bad ...'

'... so flagrant and so atrocious, that it would consequently amount to a crime ...'

'... truly exceptionally bad and so reprehensible as to justify the conclusion that it amounted to gross negligence ...'

Figure 5.6: Meaning of gross negligence

Key term: gross negligence

This is distinct from the tort concept of negligence as it relates to conduct that is 'so bad it should be characterised as criminal'.

As you can see, what we are looking for here is much more than mere negligence, something that goes 'beyond a mere matter of compensation between subjects'. Though expert evidence as to the grossness of the breach may be heard, the jury are the ultimate arbiters of whether the conduct is grossly negligent.

Summary: what do we know about gross negligence manslaughter?	
What do we mean by 'duty of care'?	A duty of care is a civil law concept, applied to the criminal law. Commonly a duty is owed as a result of the relationship between the parties. If D does not perform a positive act, it must first be proved that they owed a duty to act, before then considering whether they owed a duty of care.
When will an individual 'breach' their duty?	Breach of duty is determined according to whether D fell below the standard expected of him.
What is the 'risk' involved in the breach?	There must be a 'serious and obvious risk' of death from D's negligence. The reasonable person must stand in the shoes of D and assess whether, at that time, a serious and obvious risk of death existed.
The breach of duty must have caused the victim's death. What does this mean?	D must be both the factual and legal cause of death; his conduct must accelerate death.
When will D's negligence be 'grossly criminal'?	Grossness is a question of fact for the jury, who must consider whether the conduct of D was so bad in all the circumstances as to amount, in their judgment, to a criminal act or omission.

■ KEY POINT CHECKLIST

This chapter has covered the following key knowledge points. You can use these to structure your revision, ensuring you recall the key details for each point.

• Murder is a common law offence that requires an unlawful killing of a human being under the King's peace, where the defendant intends to kill or intends to cause serious harm.

• Loss of self-control is a partial defence to murder (and murder alone) where a defendant has suffered a loss of self-control that has arisen from a qualifying trigger (or a combination of the triggers) where the reasonable person would, in the same circumstances, have responded in the same or a similar way.

- Diminished responsibility is also a partial defence to murder (and murder alone) that requires the defendant to establish, to the civil standard, that they suffered from an abnormality of mental functioning, which arose from a recognised medical condition and has substantially impaired his ability to understand his conduct, form a rational judgment or exercise self-control. The abnormality must have caused, or significantly contributed, to the killing.

- Unlawful act manslaughter is a form of involuntary manslaughter that constructs liability for manslaughter from a criminal offence that is objectively dangerous and causes death.

- Gross negligence manslaughter is a form of involuntary manslaughter that arises when a duty of care owed to the victim has been breached, causing death. The breach must pose a serious and obvious risk of death and the defendant's conduct must be capable of being characterised as grossly negligent.

■ KEY TERMS AND CONCEPTS

- murder (**page 96**)
- malice aforethought (**page 97**)
- loss of self-control (**page 100**)
- diminished responsibility (**page 104**)
- unlawful act manslaughter (**page 108**)
- dangerousness (**page 110**)
- gross negligence manslaughter (**page 112**)
- gross negligence (**page 115**)

■ SQE1-STYLE QUESTIONS

QUESTION 1

A woman has returned home to find her boyfriend having sex with her mother. The mother jumped up and told the woman that the boyfriend had forced himself on her and threatened to hurt the woman if she did not 'lie still and take it'. The woman rushed from the room and returned with a knife from the kitchen. Seeing the knife, the boyfriend ran from the room and the woman chased him down the stairs, eventually catching him at the front door and stabbing him in the back. That single wound caused his death. The woman has been charged with murder and is claiming loss of control. She has been advised that she will not succeed with the defence as her loss of control arose as a result of the boyfriend's sexual infidelity.

Has the woman been advised correctly?

A. Yes, sexual infidelity cannot be the thing 'done or said' for the purpose of a qualifying trigger and this is the case here.

B. Yes, although there are other factors here (the alleged rape), the fact that the circumstances amount to infidelity mean that the woman is barred from raising the defence.

C. No, where sexual infidelity is an essential part of the context, it is not to be excluded in a determination of whether other things 'said and done' were grave enough to amount to the trigger.

D. No, the defence can be satisfied by evidence of any provocative conduct.

E. No, sexual infidelity can be the sole thing 'done or said' for the purpose of the qualifying trigger.

QUESTION 2

A man returned home to find a woman in his property. He confronted the woman and asked, 'What do you think you are doing?' The woman responded by hitting the man with the torch she was holding, intending to cause him serious injury. The man died as a result of that injury and the woman was charged with murder. At trial, the woman asserted that she had lost self-control as she had felt a justifiable sense of being seriously wronged when the man had questioned what she was doing. The trial judge concluded that there was insufficient evidence of a qualifying trigger to leave the defence of loss of control to the jury.

Is the judge entitled to make this decision?

A. Yes, there must be evidence satisfying both the fear trigger and the anger trigger before the defence can be left to the jury.

B. No, the defence must always be left to the jury where there is some evidence that a trigger or triggers will be satisfied.

C. No, the focus is upon whether the woman felt a justifiable sense of being seriously wronged and the jury should have been directed to assess this.

D. Yes, the judge is entitled to withdraw the defence from the jury if he has concluded that there is insufficient evidence of a qualifying trigger.

E. No, even if there is insufficient evidence of a qualifying trigger the woman is entitled to argue she has been otherwise provoked into the killing.

QUESTION 3

A woman has been caring for her husband for 20 years. The husband suffers from dementia and his condition has worsened in the past year. The woman is older than her husband and is concerned that, when she dies, he will not be cared for properly. One afternoon, the woman takes her husband into the garden and gives him a cup of tea that she has adulterated with her pain medication. She intends to bring about his swift and painless death and the tea has the desired result. The woman has been charged with his murder and seeks advice as to whether her concern about her husband's welfare can form the basis of a plea of diminished responsibility.

Can the woman argue diminished responsibility?

A. Yes, diminished responsibility provides a partial defence for those who are morally deserving of it.

B. Yes, the woman need only prove, to the civil standard, that her concern about his welfare had prevented her from making a rational decision.

C. No, the woman's concern about her husband's welfare falls short of a recognised mental condition.

D. No, the woman would have to provide evidence that proved beyond reasonable doubt that she satisfied the elements of the defence, and this is unlikely on the facts.

E. Yes, a jury do not need to hear any medical evidence pertaining to any specific medical condition.

QUESTION 4

A boy, aged 12, has been teased at school after his mum decided to give him a haircut at home. One girl in his class had spent all day laughing and pointing at the boy. The boy corners the girl outside the school and shows her a flick knife (where the blade is hidden inside the handle and springs out when a button is pressed), telling her, 'Let's see how you look if I cut off all your hair.' The girl struggled to escape, and the boy's finger pressed against the button, the blade flew out and entered the girl's throat. The girl died of blood loss and the boy was charged with unlawful act manslaughter. On the question of dangerousness, the trial judge directed the jury that 'you must ask yourselves whether a reasonable 12-year-old boy would have seen an inevitable risk of some harm'.

Have the jury been correctly directed?

A. Yes, the jury can take into account the age of the boy.

B. Yes, the reasonable person is afforded all relevant characteristics of the boy.

C. No, the test requires foresight of an inevitable risk of serious harm.

D. No, the age of the boy is irrelevant to the test of dangerousness.

E. No, the test is subjective, and the jury should be asked whether the boy appreciated that there was an inevitable risk of some harm.

QUESTION 5

A woman, a general practitioner (GP), has started work at a new practice and is reading the introductory literature they have provided her with. In that literature, it states that all GPs need to ensure that they keep up to date with developments in medicine as 'if they fail to diagnose a patient and that patient dies, this will be in breach of their duty of care, even where that condition and/or symptoms are not widely recognised as serious. A jury may then find them liable for gross negligence manslaughter.' The woman does not believe that this is true.

Is this an accurate statement of the law?

A. Yes, the offence of gross negligence manslaughter merely requires that a defendant breaches their duty of care.

B. No, there must be an obvious and serious risk of harm at the time of the breach.

C. No, there must be an obvious and serious risk of death at the time of the breach.

D. No, gross negligence cannot be based upon an omission.

E. Yes, as a jury can take account of developments in medicine that a reasonably competent doctor would not have been aware of.

■ ANSWERS TO QUESTIONS

Answers to 'What do you know already?' questions at the start of the chapter

1) The mens rea for murder is the intention to kill or cause GBH. Importantly, the offence is not restricted to intention to kill; an intention to cause GBH is also acceptable.
2) True. The loss of control need not be sudden, though it must be actual.
3) False. A defendant who raises the partial defence of diminished responsibility must prove the existence of that offence.
4) To be liable for the offence of unlawful act manslaughter the defendant must satisfy the base offence (the identified criminal offence), which may have particular requirements relating to foresight of harm. However, in terms of dangerousness, the test is objective, and the question is whether the reasonable person would see an inevitable risk of some harm.
5) Various epithets have been used to describe what amounts to gross negligence and a jury should be directed using language that reflects the fact that the conduct must be exceptionally bad in order to justify a finding of gross negligence.

Answers to end-of-chapter SQE1-style questions

Question 1:
   The correct answer was C. The exclusion of sexual infidelity does not mean that other things 'said and done' cannot be taken into consideration for the purpose of establishing a qualifying trigger. Options A and B are incorrect as they fail to understand the circumstances where sexual infidelity can be relevant. Option D is incorrect as there is no qualifying trigger related to mere 'provocative conduct'. Option E is incorrect as it ignores the exclusion of sexual infidelity as a sole qualifying trigger in the legislation.

Question 2:
   The correct answer was D. The judge is required to carefully review the evidence to establish whether there is sufficient evidence amounting to a qualifying trigger (therefore option B is incorrect). Option A is incorrect as the defence need only establish the 'anger' or the 'fear' trigger, not both. Option C misstates the test as a subjective one, as opposed to an objective test. Option E is a simple misstatement of the law – there must be an evidential basis for pleading the defence.

Question 3:

The correct answer was C. The defence requires the woman to be suffering from a recognised medical condition and there is no indication here that this is the case (option E is therefore wrong as medical evidence would need to be submitted to support the defence). Option A is wrong because the defence does not operate to benefit those who are morally deserving. Option B is wrong because there has to be a recognised medical condition that caused the disease of the mind; her concern for his wellbeing is not such a recognised condition. Option D is incorrect as, while the burden of proof is on the defence to prove the existence of the defence, this is on the civil standard of proof and not the criminal standard.

Question 4:

The correct answer was D. The test for dangerousness is an objective one (therefore option E is wrong). The age of the accused will be relevant to the question of whether they had the mens rea for the unlawful act but not for the estimation of dangerousness (therefore while option A is technically correct, it is not the most accurate answer). Option B is also wrong for the same reason – the reasonable person would be aware of the same circumstances as the boy, but will not share their characteristics when determining dangerousness. Option C is wrong because it misstates the test as being foresight of 'serious harm' – the test is whether there is foresight of 'some harm'.

Question 5:

The correct answer was C. There must be a breach of duty and this can be by way of an omission (therefore option D is wrong), but at the time of the breach there must be an obvious and serious risk of death (therefore options A and B are incorrect). Option E is wrong as the assessment must be made based on the information available to the reasonable man standing in the shoes of the woman.

■ KEY CASES, RULES, STATUTES AND INSTRUMENTS

The SQE1 Assessment Specification does not require you to know any case names or statutory materials for the topic of homicide. Despite this, you are strongly advised to read s 2 HA 1957 (diminished responsibility) and s 54–56 CJA 2009 (loss of control) in full, and the associated case law interpreting those statutes. Murder and involuntary manslaughter are common law offences, so you are advised to read into any principles discussed here in further detail.

6

Non-fatal offences against the person

■ MAKE SURE YOU KNOW

This chapter will cover the core principles of non-fatal offences against the person. For the purposes of SQE1, you must understand the offences of assault, battery, assault occasioning actual bodily harm (ABH), wounding/inflicting grievous bodily harm (GBH), and wounding/causing GBH with intent. You are required to know each offence in turn and be able to identify and apply the relevant law appropriately and effectively to realistic client-based problems and situations.

The SQE1 Assessment Specification has not identified that candidates are required to recall/recite any case names for the topic of non-fatal offences. It does identify, however, that candidates must know ss 47, 20 and 18 of the Offences Against the Person Act (OAPA) 1861. It is likely that a multiple-choice question (MCQ) may be asked making direct reference to the statutory number, as opposed to the name of the offence itself. For example, it is likely that you may be asked whether a 's 47 offence has been committed' as opposed to whether 'an offence of assault occasioning ABH has been committed'.

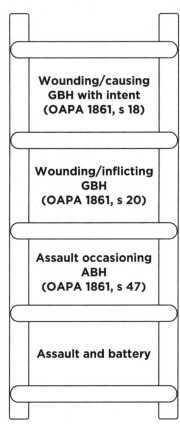

Wounding/causing
GBH with intent
(OAPA 1861, s 18)

Wounding/inflicting
GBH
(OAPA 1861, s 20)

Assault occasioning
ABH
(OAPA 1861, s 47)

Assault and battery

Overview of non-fatal offences against the person

■ SQE ASSESSMENT ADVICE

As you work through this chapter, remember to pay particular attention in your revision to:
• the distinction between the offences of common assault and battery
• how consent operates
• the elements that must be proven to establish a s 47 offence
• the elements that must be proven to establish a s 20 offence
• the elements that must be proven to establish a s 18 offence.

■ WHAT DO YOU KNOW ALREADY?

Have a go at these questions before reading this chapter. If you find some difficult or cannot remember the answers, make a note to look more closely at that area during your revision.

1) What actus reus elements must be proven to establish an assault?
   [Assault, pages 125–129]
2) True or false: for a battery to take place the victim must suffer physical injury.
   [Battery, pages 129–131]
3) Fill in the blank: the mens rea for assault occasioning ABH is _____.
   [Assault occasioning ABH (OAPA 1861, s 47), pages 134–137]
4) To satisfy s 20 does the defendant have to foresee that a wound or GBH will result?
   [Wounding/inflicting GBH (OAPA 1861, s 20), pages 137–141]
5) Is s 18 an offence of basic intent or specific intent?
   [Wounding or GBH, with intent (OAPA 1861, s 18), pages 141–143]

INTRODUCTION TO NON-FATAL OFFENCES AGAINST THE PERSON

The offences that will be discussed in this chapter are often referred to by a ladder of non-fatal offences (see the **opening figure**).

Assault and battery (commonly referred to together as 'common assault') are common law offences and the actus reus and mens rea of these offences have been established in case law. An assault is sometimes termed a technical or psychic assault in order to distinguish it from battery. We will use the terms 'assault' and 'battery'.

The OAPA 1861 prescribes a number of statutory offences, namely:
• assault/battery occasioning ABH (OAPA 1861, s 47)
• inflicting GBH or malicious wounding (OAPA 1861, s 20)
• causing GBH or wounding, with intent (OAPA 1861, s 18).

One key distinction between the common-law offences and the more serious statutory offences is that the common-law offences do not require any resultant harm. If harm has been caused, then the statutory offences should be considered. The terminology may, at first, appear confusing. The remainder of this chapter, however, will proceed to discuss these offences in greater detail.

ASSAULT

The first offence to consider is **assault**.

Key term: assault
An assault is any act that intentionally – or possibly recklessly – causes another person to apprehend immediate and unlawful personal violence.

The offence of assault can therefore be broken down into four elements, as shown in **Figure 6.1** (overleaf).

Please note, the terms 'harm' or 'force' are sometimes used in place of 'violence'.

Apprehension

The requirement that the defendant 'causes another person to apprehend' necessitates an examination of the 'other person's' response to the situation. For example, if Mark jokingly points a gun at Sam (his

D must cause another person to **apprehend** harm

The apprehension must be of **immediate** harm

The apprehension must be of **unlawful personal violence**

D must **intend or be reckless** as to causing the victim to apprehend unlawful and immediate personal violence

Figure 6.1: Elements of assault

friend) and pulls the trigger, Sam will not expect violence to be applied to her if she has examined the gun and has established there are no bullets.

These were the facts in *R v Lamb* [1967] 2 QB 981, and these facts were discussed in the context of unlawful act manslaughter in **Chapter 5**.

The same could be said for an individual who is unaware that they are about to be struck. Suppose Sam, for example, rushes up behind Mark and pushes him. Mark was unaware of Sam's presence. In this case, there is no assault as Mark could not have apprehended harm from Sam (though, of course, there will be a battery).

Apprehension is not the same, though, as 'fear'; a victim need not be fearful of harm in order for an offence to be made out. It is sufficient that the individual, although not afraid, expects that force will be applied (see **Practice example 6.1**).

Practice example 6.1

Frank pointed a gun at Jessica. The weapon he was holding was an imitation firearm and Frank was acting in jest, but Jessica was not aware that the weapon was an imitation firearm and ran away.
Has an assault been committed?

These are similar facts to *Logdon v DPP* [1976] Crim LR 121. The Divisional Court held that there was an assault as the victim had apprehended that violence was going to be applied to her. It did not matter that there was no possibility of the perceived threat being carried out. The focus was on what the victim thought was going to happen.

Immediacy

An expectation of 'immediate and unlawful personal violence' suggests close proximity between the defendant and his victim, a typical example being where one person stands in front of another with raised fists. The courts have, however, been willing to stretch the meaning of immediacy to embrace situations where the aggressor and the victim are not proximate.

Consider the following examples:

a) A man stands outside of the window of a home, looking in at the resident.

b) A man calls a woman on her phone and does not speak.

c) A man posts abusive letters to a woman's home address.

In all the above circumstances, it is possible to find that the victim expects an **immediate** application of force. In the first example, the Divisional Court held that force could be applied sufficiently immediately, despite the door being locked. In the second and third examples, it was accepted that where violence could be used against a person within 'a minute or two', this could amount to an assault.

Key term: immediate
'Immediate' not only includes where violence can be applied to the person there and then, but also where it can be applied imminently.

Exam warning
It is important that the actus reus of the offence is correctly stated. If you were to say that the victim must 'immediately apprehend an application of violence' this would be incorrect, as it suggests that violence could be used against the victim at some point in the future. The offence requires that the victim apprehends that violence will be used against them immediately. See **Figure 6.2** for further clarity.

'Apprehension of immediate harm'	• This is the **correct** statement of law. • The harm *itself* must be immediately apprehended.
'Immediate apprehension of harm'	• This is the **incorrect** statement of law. • This would allow for an individual to claim that they immediately apprehended harm which may take place in the future.

Figure 6.2: Confusion over the use of 'immediacy'

Unlawful personal violence

Unlawfulness is dealt with in **Table 6.3**, but simply means 'without consent' or 'without lawful excuse'.

The victim must apprehend that violence will be applied to their person. An apprehension of violence may sound extreme, but it merely requires an expectation of non-consensual contact. This can be as insignificant as a light touch, or as substantial as a punch. There is no requirement that the victim feels that any contact has been made. Indeed, if such contact is made, the relevant offence would be that of battery (discussed below).

Intention or recklessness

The mens rea of assault requires the defendant to either intend to cause, or be reckless as to causing, the victim to apprehend the application of immediate and unlawful violence. Intention means, as discussed in **Chapter 1**, that it is the defendant's aim or purpose to bring about the prohibited result. As recklessness is an alternative here, it is not necessary to consider oblique intention. Furthermore, you must remember that 'recklessness' means subjective recklessness (see **Chapter 1**).

Additional points on assault

Some final questions on assault are dealt with in **Table 6.1**. Consider whether you know the answer to the question first, and then see the answer provided.

Table 6.1: Additional questions on assault

Question	Answer
Does an assault have to be committed by way of an act?	No, so long as there was a recognised duty to act, D can be liable for his failure to act (see **Chapter 1**).
Can you assault by words alone?	Yes: 'A thing said is also a thing done' (per Lord Steyn in *R v Ireland*).
Is it sufficient for a person to fear unlawful force will be applied to him immediately?	The requirement is that the victim 'apprehends' the unlawful application of immediate force. In many cases this will be satisfied if he 'fears' it. However, there must be an expectation or anticipation that the force will be applied.

Summary: what do we know about assault?

What does it mean to say that the victim must 'apprehend' the application of force?	'Apprehension' does not refer to fear, per se; rather, it refers to an expectation on the part of the victim that they will be subjected to harm.
What is the requirement of 'immediacy'?	The apprehension must be of 'immediate unlawful personal violence'. This does not mean instantaneous and can be understood to mean 'imminent' (ie in a minute or two).
What is 'unlawful personal violence'?	'Unlawful' means without consent or unjustified. 'Personal' means force being applied to the person, as opposed to their property, for example.
	'Violence' does not require any harm to be suffered and the victim may apprehend even the slightest touch.
What is the mens rea for assault?	D must either intend to cause the victim to apprehend harm, or be reckless as to such apprehension occurring.

BATTERY

Formally known as 'assault by beating', **battery** is a straightforward offence.

Key term: battery

Battery is an act by which the defendant, intentionally or recklessly, applies unlawful force to the victim.

Therefore, while assault is the apprehension of harm, battery is the physical application of that harm. The offence of battery can be broken down into three elements (see **Figure 6.3** overleaf).

An application

There must be physical contact for battery to be made out. Although an assault will often precede a battery, for example where a person sees that they are about to be punched, this is not a prerequisite. There will still be a battery where Mark punches Sam in the back of the head or pushes a blind person. Force may also be applied through an object, such as a weapon.

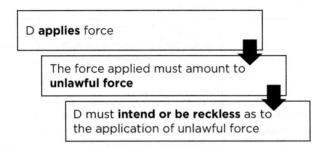

Figure 6.3: Elements of battery

The application of force need not be direct. Consider the examples in **Table 6.2**.

Table 6.2: Examples of indirect force

Example
D punched a woman, causing her to drop the baby she was holding. The baby hit the floor. D was charged with battery of the child and convicted. He appealed on the grounds that the force was insufficiently direct. The Divisional Court rejected this argument. His application of force to the woman had resulted in force being applied to the baby. *Haystead v Chief Constable of Derbyshire* [2000] 3 All ER 890
D blocked the exit door in a theatre and shouted 'fire', resulting in the theatregoers rushing to the exit to escape. Several were crushed in the ensuing rush against the door. *R v Martin* (1881) 8 QBD 54

In both incidences, force has been applied to the person, albeit indirectly. The application of force may also arise by way of an omission. As discussed in **Chapter 1**, where the application of force flows from an omission, the defendant must be under a duty to act.

Unlawful violence

Unlawfulness will be discussed below, but violence merely means any unlawful contact with the person, whether or not that contact is felt.

There is no need to show hostility or malice on behalf of the defendant. There is no requirement to prove that any injury has been suffered.

Intention or recklessness
The mens rea of battery requires that the defendant intends or is subjectively reckless as to the application of unlawful violence.

Summary: what do we know about battery?	
What is 'battery'?	Battery is where unlawful force is applied to the person. That application can be direct, indirect or by an omission.
Is there a requirement for harm in order to prove that battery has taken place?	There is no requirement that harm need result from an assault or a battery, nor need D foresee any harm.

UNLAWFULNESS
You will have noted that force, whether anticipated (assault) or applied (battery), must be 'unlawful'. An application of force may be lawful in certain circumstances and you must be aware of how consent operates.

Exam warning
Self-defence is also relevant here and you do need to be aware of how self-defence may operate to make an application of force lawful. Self-defence is discussed in **Chapter 4**.

Consent
Where a person makes consensual contact with another (eg by shaking hands), this will not amount to a battery. In these cases, consent to that contact will normally make that application of force lawful. The same principle applies when, for example, you consent to surgery or to participate in sports.

For consent to be effective, a number of conditions must be fulfilled (see **Table 6.3**).

Some final questions on consent are dealt with in **Table 6.4**. Consider whether you know the answer to the question first, and then see the answer provided.

Table 6.3: Summary of effective consent

Conditions	Explanation and examples
Consent must be express or implied	Implied consent is given to everyday activities such as handshakes, a congratulatory pat on the back or being jostled on public transport.
	Express consent is where a person overtly indicates that they are consenting. For example, opening your arms to embrace another person, visiting the doctor for a check-up or signing a form to consent to a piercing.
The party giving consent must have the capacity, freedom and be fully informed in order to give effective consent	A person may not have capacity to consent if they have a permanent or temporary mental disorder or are insufficiently mature. Furthermore, this party must not be acting under duress (ie under force).
	In addition, consent must be fully informed. The courts have made clear that the activity in question, and any harm that may result, must be taken into consideration in assessing whether sufficient information has been given.
Where consent has been induced by fraud it is not effective consent	Fraud may negate consent if it relates to: • The identity of D. This includes a fraud as to personal identity (ie impersonating Mr X when you are Mr Y) and a deception about qualifications and attributes that go to the heart of your identity, such as being a qualified medical doctor. This is narrowly interpreted. • The nature or quality of the act. For example, where V consents to a physical examination that they are told is for a medical purpose, but is instead sexually motivated.
The party providing the consent must be legally entitled to consent to the activity	Consent can be given to what would otherwise amount to an assault or a battery (*R v Brown* [1994] 1 AC 212).
	Where ABH (see s 47 below) is intended or risked, consent is irrelevant unless there is good reason for that harm to be caused.
	Activities exempted on the grounds of good reason include: • regulated sporting activities • reasonable surgical interference • rough horseplay

continued

Table 6.3: Continued

Conditions	Explanation and examples
	• tattooing and piercing • male circumcision • dangerous performances and religious flagellation Bodily harm (including serious bodily harm) can be risked in the course of sexual activity if the consent given is fully informed and the sexual activity is not violent.

Table 6.4: Additional questions on consent

Question	Answer
Can D avoid liability if they have a mistaken but genuine belief in consent?	Yes, though evidence of a genuine belief in effective consent must be adduced by D.
Is D still liable where consent has been given to a battery that results in ABH, which had been neither intended nor foreseen by D?	D will not be liable for s 47 (below) if effective consent has been given to the battery and the injury is unforeseen.
Can a person consent to intentional bodily harm during sexual activity?	No. By virtue of *R v Brown*, if the injury results from violent sexual activity then effective consent cannot be given. If the injury results from non-violent sexual activity then you can consent to the risk of injury, but not the certainty.

THE STATUTORY OFFENCES

The next section will consider three offences found in the OAPA 1861.

Revision tip

The SQE1 Assessment Specification has identified that candidates must know and be able to use ss 47, 20 and 18 OAPA 1861. For your purposes, this means that you may face an MCQ where the question includes a statutory provision, or where the answer options include such a provision. You must understand what each statutory provision refers to, for example assault occasioning ABH is also known as a **'s 47 offence'**.

ASSAULT OCCASIONING ABH (OAPA 1861, S 47)

A **s 47 offence** is the least serious of the statutory non-fatal offences.

> ### Key term: s 47 offence
>
> A s 47 offence is, in essence, an aggravated assault. The offence requires the prosecution to prove an assault or battery that causes ABH.

The **s 47 offence** can therefore be broken down into the three elements summarised in **Figure 6.4**.

Each of these will be addressed in turn.

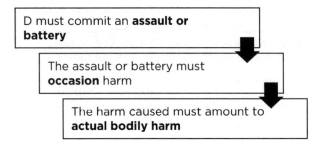

Figure 6.4: Elements of ABH

Assault or battery

First, the defendant must commit an assault or a battery. Despite the name '*assault* occasioning ABH', either of these common law offences can be used to construct liability for the offence and these are sometimes referred to as the 'base offence'. The assault or the battery must first be established in full – that is, that the actus reus and the mens rea must be proved. Importantly, the only mens rea requirement for s 47 is that for the assault or the battery, there is no additional mens rea relating to the injury suffered.

> ### Exam warning
>
> A common mistake made by candidates is to consider that D must intend or be reckless to causing ABH. This is not the case; the *mens rea* for ABH is simply the same as the *mens rea* for assault or battery (whichever is relevant in your case). Look out for this in an MCQ that attempts to suggest that D did not intend to cause injury (see **Practice example 6.2**).

Practice example 6.2

Sandy was in a car being driven to a party. The driver had made several sexual overtures to Sandy and had asked her to undress. When he leant over and tugged at the hem of her coat she jumped out of the moving car. As a result, Sandy suffered a broken ankle and the driver was convicted of a s 47 offence. The driver asserted that he could not be liable for assault occasioning ABH as he had not intended, nor had he foreseen, that his passenger would be injured.

Can the driver avoid liability as he did not have foresight of harm?

These were the facts of *R v Roberts* (1972) 56 Cr App R 95. The Court of Appeal held that there was no need to prove mens rea in relation to the harm caused; it was sufficient he had the mens rea for the battery.

If an assault or battery cannot be proven there can be no liability for s 47 assault occasioning ABH.

Occasioning

This is the causal element and requires that the defendant has brought about (caused) both the result element of the assault or the battery, and the ABH. This requires a consideration of factual causation, legal causation and the rules relating to new and intervening acts (see **Chapter 1**).

ABH

ABH is injury that is more than 'transient and trifling', that is to say it is more than minimal injury, but not so serious as to amount to GBH (see **Figure 6.5**).

Bruising that is more than transient and trifling would amount to ABH, as would scratches, burns, swelling and grazes (see **Practice example 6.3**).

Practice example 6.3

Fiona had split up with her boyfriend. One evening, he restrained her and cut off her ponytail. He caused no additional harm to her person. He was charged with assault occasioning ABH contrary to s 47 of the OAPA 1861. The magistrates' court held that there was no case to answer in relation to this charge, as the cutting of hair did not amount to ABH.

Was the magistrates' court correct to hold that this could not amount to ABH?

These were the facts of *DPP v Smith* [2006] EWHC 94 (Admin). On appeal, Sir Igor Judge P held that hair is part of the body and cutting it could amount to ABH. It would clearly have to be – as was the case here – a substantial portion of the hair to amount to harm that is more than transient and trifling (though any cutting of hair could amount to a battery, if not ABH).

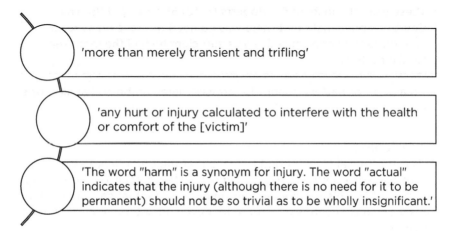

'more than merely transient and trifling'

'any hurt or injury calculated to interfere with the health or comfort of the [victim]'

'The word "harm" is a synonym for injury. The word "actual" indicates that the injury (although there is no need for it to be permanent) should not be so trivial as to be wholly insignificant.'

Figure 6.5: Meaning of ABH

Psychiatric harm

The OAPA 1861 speaks only of 'bodily harm'. In *R v Chan-Fook* [1994] 2 All ER 552, the Court of Appeal accepted that 'bodily harm' should be interpreted to include psychiatric harm. Some final questions on psychiatric harm are dealt with in **Table 6.5**. Consider whether you know the answer to the question first, and then see the answer provided.

Exam warning

You may be aware of the Crown Prosecution (CPS) Charging Standards. While these provide some useful examples of the injuries that amount to ABH, GBH, etc, the Charging Standards are there to assist prosecutors, they do not represent the substantive law.

Table 6.5: Additional questions on psychiatric harm

Question	Answer
Does panic or fear amount to ABH?	No, while ABH includes psychiatric injury it does not include mere emotions such as fear, distress or panic, nor does it include, as such, states of mind that are not themselves evidence of some identifiable clinical condition.
Does psychiatric harm have to be foreseen by D for the s 47 offence to be proven?	No, D only needs mens rea in relation to the assault or the battery.
Does this mean that an assault that causes V to suffer depression will always amount to s 47?	It may amount to ABH, but only where the injury falls short of serious injury.

Summary: what do we know about the s 47 offence?	
What must be proven for the offence of assault occasioning ABH?	It must be proven that D committed an assault or battery, which caused another person to suffer ABH. D need not intend or be reckless to causing such harm; the mens rea is the same as the mens rea for assault and battery.
What does 'occasioning' mean?	'Occasioning' simply means to cause (ie factual and legal causation – see **Chapter 1**).
What is the meaning of 'ABH'?	ABH is harm that is more than transient and trifling.

WOUNDING/INFLICTING GBH (OAPA 1861, S 20)

The next offence to be considered is a **s 20 offence**.

Key term: s 20 offence
Section 20 OAPA 1861 criminalises the infliction of GBH and/or malicious wounding, where D intends or is reckless as to some bodily harm.

The s 20 offence can be broken down into the two elements shown in **Figure 6.6**.

D must unlawfully **wound** or **inflict GBH**

D must **intend** to cause some harm, or be **reckless** to the thought of some harm

Figure 6.6: Elements of s 20

As you can see, there are two alternative versions of the actus reus here: (a) wounding and (b) inflicting GBH.

Exam warning

Please remember that wounding and GBH are alternatives. You need only establish a wound or GBH. Make sure you avoid coming to the wrong conclusion in an MCQ.

Wounding

To amount to a wound in law two factors must be fulfilled:
• the skin must be broken, and
• that break in the skin must be through both layers – the dermis and the epidermis.

Injuries that will not amount to a wound include:
• a scratch that does not break both layers of the skin
• the rupture of a blood vessel
• a broken bone that has not broken through the skin.

A wound can be as minor as a pinprick that goes through both layers of the skin, or as extreme as a serious stab wound. If a wound is serious it may also amount to GBH.

Wounding will typically be by way of a direct application of force (eg by stabbing V with a knife). There is no direct authority on whether wounding can be caused indirectly, although as the courts have found that GBH can be inflicted indirectly, it is likely that the same principle applies to wounding.

Inflicting GBH

Two terms require further consideration: (i) inflicting and (ii) GBH.

Inflicting

'Inflicting' is synonymous with 'cause' and requires the tests for causation to be considered (see **Practice example 6.4**).

Practice example 6.4

Katy broke off her relationship with Jed. Jed was unhappy with this decision and harassed Katy by way of silent telephone calls. He also distributed offensive cards in her street, took photographs of her and sent her abusive notes in the post. Katy was frightened and fearful as a result of this campaign of harassment and was diagnosed as suffering from a serious depressive illness. Jed was convicted of inflicting GBH contrary to s 20.

Can we say Jed has 'inflicted' GBH upon Katy?

These facts reflect those of *Burstow* (heard as the co-joined appeal of *R v Ireland; R v Burstow* [1998] AC 147). The House of Lords held that 'one can nowadays quite naturally speak of inflicting psychiatric injury'. If 'inflict' were more narrowly construed it would lead to the ridiculous situation that liability could be found for s 18 – if GBH were intended – but not the lesser offence at s 20 where it was risked.

GBH

Whether **GBH** has been suffered is a question of fact for the jury who, in reaching their decision, can take into account:
- the totality of the injuries if a number of minor injuries have been suffered
- the age and health of the victim, and any other relevant factors.

Key term: GBH

GBH means 'really serious bodily harm'. The courts have held that the word 'really' adds nothing to the definition and it would not be a misdirection to omit the word 'really'.

The principles described above do little to assist our practical understanding of what injuries may be sufficiently serious to amount to GBH. This is better illustrated through some examples from the case law:
- A broken collar bone amounted to GBH.
- GBH was inflicted through the transmission of HIV.
- Severe depression amounted to GBH.
- Body modifications including the removal of an ear and a tongue bifurcation were treated as GBH.

Intention or recklessness

The offence in s 20 OAPA 1861 merely tells us that the defendant must wound or inflict GBH 'maliciously'. 'Maliciously' simply refers to the mens rea requirement for s 20.

For a s 20 offence, the defendant must intend or be subjectively reckless so as to cause 'some harm'. There is no requirement for the defendant to intend or be reckless as to wounding or causing GBH (see **Practice example 6.5**).

Practice example 6.5
A man breaks the leg of his infant son by handling him roughly. He is charged with an offence contrary to s 20 and the trial judge directs the jury that they could find the man liable for that offence if he should have foreseen the risk that his handling of the child would result in some harm. The man was convicted.
On what ground can the man appeal his conviction?
These are the facts of *R v Savage; DPP v Parmenter* [1992] 1 AC 699, where the Court of Appeal held that there had been a misdirection by the trial judge. It is not sufficient to ask whether D should have foreseen a risk of injury, as that is an objective test. The correct direction would have been to ask whether D had actually foreseen that some harm would result.

Summary: what do we know about the s 20 offence?	
What is the offence under s 20 OAPA 1861?	D may be liable in circumstances where he maliciously wounds the victim or inflicts GBH.
What is the meaning of a 'wound'?	A wound is a break in both layers of the skin.
What is the meaning of 'GBH'?	GBH simply means 'serious harm'. In deciding whether it amounts to serious harm the jury can consider the totality of injuries (where relevant) and the victim characteristics.
What is the mens rea for a s 20 offence?	D must intend to cause *some harm*, or be reckless as to some harm being caused.

WOUNDING OR GBH, WITH INTENT (OAPA 1861, S 18)

The final offence to be considered is a **s 18 offence.**

Key term: s 18 offence

A s 18 offence is the most serious offence considered in this chapter. The actus reus for a s 18 offence is identical to that of s 20 considered above; the distinction between a s 20 offence and a s 18 offence is the mens rea. While s 20 can be satisfied by proof of recklessness, s 18 may only be committed with an intention.

The s 18 offence can therefore be broken down into two elements, as shown in **Figure 6.7.**

Each of these will be addressed in turn.

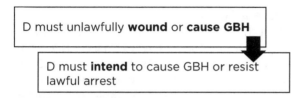

Figure 6.7: Elements of s 18

Wounding or GBH

Section 18 requires a 'wound' or 'GBH' to be caused. Both wounding and GBH have the same meaning as in s 20. 'Causing' carries the same meaning as 'occasioning' in s 47 and 'infliction' in s 20, and should be assessed by reference to the ordinary principles of causation.

Intention to cause GBH or resist lawful arrest

Section 18 is a specific-intent offence. This means that it can only be committed with intention (recklessness is not sufficient).

The mens rea for s 18 is alternative, requiring the defendant to either:
• intend to cause GBH, or
• intend to resist or prevent lawful arrest.

We can take each of these alternatives in turn.

Intention to cause GBH

The first alternative is that the defendant intends to cause GBH. **Table 6.6** outlines some of the fundamental features of this form of intention.

Table 6.6: Intention to cause GBH

Principle	Explanation
Level of harm intended	Unlike s 20, which requires D to intend only *some* harm, a s 18 offence requires the prosecution to prove that D intended to cause serious harm (ie GBH).
Is an intention to wound sufficient?	An intention to wound is not sufficient for a s 18 offence. Even if the actus reus alleged is wounding, the mens rea required is that D intended to cause GBH. There is no offence of 'wounding with intent to wound'.
Relevance of the word 'maliciously'	If D is charged with 'maliciously causing GBH with intent to do GBH' then 'malicious' adds nothing. If you intend to cause GBH you are clearly malicious as to the causing of GBH.

Intention to resist or prevent lawful arrest

The second alternative is that the defendant intends to resist or prevent lawful arrest. **Table 6.6** demonstrated that the word 'maliciously' adds nothing where the mens rea alleged is an intention to cause GBH. However, where the intention alleged is to resist or prevent lawful apprehension, maliciousness has some relevance. **Table 6.7** outlines some of the fundamental features of this form of intention.

Remember that these mens rea are alternative; the prosecution does not need to establish both.

Table 6.7: Intention to resist or prevent lawful arrest

Principle	Explanation
What do we mean by 'resist or prevent lawful arrest'?	D can be liable for GBH where he causes a wound or GBH in the process of resisting or preventing lawful arrest. In circumstances where D lacks the intention to cause harm but does possess the intention to prevent lawful arrest, a s 18 offence can be made out. Importantly, the arrest must be 'lawful' – if the arrest is unlawful, then this form of alternative mens rea cannot be relied upon.
Relevance of the word 'maliciously'	If D is charged with 'maliciously causing GBH intending to resist or prevent the lawful apprehension or detainer of any person' and it is proven that he intended to resist or prevent an arrest, it then also needs to be proven that he has been reckless as to causing harm.

Summary: what do we know about the s 18 offence?	
What is the meaning of 'wounding' and 'GBH' for a s 18 offence?	Wounding and GBH bear the same meaning as for s 20.
What is the mens rea for a s 18 offence?	D must intend to cause GBH or intend to prevent or resist lawful arrest. An intention to wound is not sufficient.
What is the relevance of 'maliciousness' in s 18?	Where the prosecution allege an intention to cause GBH, the word 'maliciously' adds nothing to the offence. Where the prosecution allege an intention to resist lawful arrest, the prosecution must also prove that D was reckless as to causing some harm.

■ KEY POINT CHECKLIST

This chapter has covered the following key knowledge points. You can use these to structure your revision, ensuring you recall the key details for each point.

- Assault occurs where the victim apprehends the immediate application of unlawful force and battery is the unlawful application of that force. Both offences can be committed intentionally, or with subjective recklessness.
- Section 47 is the least serious of the statutory offences and is committed when an assault and battery causes ABH. ABH is injury that is more than minor.
- Section 20 is committed when a wound or GBH is inflicted upon another person. The defendant need only intend or be reckless that some harm will result.
- Section 18 is an intention-only offence and is committed when the defendant intends to cause GBH or intends to resist or prevent an arrest.
- Consent may act as a defence to a non-fatal offence.

■ KEY TERMS AND CONCEPTS

- assault (**page 125**)
- immediate (**page 127**)

- battery (**page 129**)
- s 47 offence (**page 134**)
- s 20 offence (**page 137**)
- GBH (**page 139**)
- s 18 offence (**page 141**)

■ SQE1-STYLE QUESTIONS

QUESTION 1

A man has been calling his ex-girlfriend on her mobile phone and hanging up before she answers. He has disguised his number, but the woman is aware that it is the man as he had told a mutual friend that he intended to 'scare her' by making the calls. The woman knows that the man is currently working 100 miles away but becomes concerned she may be at risk of violence.

Has the man committed an assault?

A. No, an assault cannot be committed by silence.

B. Yes, an assault can be committed by silence alone and if the woman is scared then an assault has been committed.

C. No, an assault requires an application of force.

D. Yes, an assault can be committed by silence and if the woman feels at risk of violence in the future an assault has been committed.

E. No, an assault can be committed by silence, but the woman does not, on the facts, expect violence to be applied to her immediately.

QUESTION 2

A man has hit a woman on the back of her head during an argument. The woman has not sustained any injuries as a result of being hit. The man has now been charged with battery.

Has the man committed a battery?

A. No, an assault must precede a battery.

B. No, injury must result for a battery to be made out.

C. Yes, the man has applied unlawful force to the woman.

D. Yes, the man has caused the woman to expect the application of unlawful force.

E. No, as the man has hit the woman on the head the appropriate offence would be s 47 OAPA 1861.

QUESTION 3

A man and a woman are in the woman's car and are travelling to pick up their children from swimming club. The man tells the woman that her children are poor swimmers and will never be chosen to represent the club in an upcoming competition. The woman is upset and intentionally shoves the man. As the car door has not been properly closed it springs open and the man falls out of the car, suffering some bruising and grazing. The woman is charged with s 47 OAPA 1861 but maintains she did not foresee that the man would suffer any injury.

Has the woman committed a s 47 offence?

A. Yes, if it can be proven that an injury was reasonably foreseeable.

B. Yes, there is no requirement that injury is foreseen.

C. No, s 47 requires serious injury to be suffered.

D. No, there must be foresight of some harm.

E. No, s 47 requires an intention to do harm.

QUESTION 4

A man and woman work together. The woman has recently made the man angry by suggesting he was not doing his job properly. One afternoon, the man saw the woman going into a small room where the office stationery was kept. To get revenge, the man decided to lock the door and trap the woman in the room. The woman spent the rest of the afternoon trapped in the small room. As a result, the woman has now been diagnosed with post-traumatic stress disorder (PTSD). The man has been charged with an offence contrary to s 20 OAPA 1861. His defence asserts that he has not inflicted harm upon the woman.

Has there been an infliction of harm?

A. Yes, an infliction is made out where there has been an assault.

B. No, an infliction requires an application of force.

C. Yes, if injury has been suffered then it is merely assumed that this has been inflicted.

D. Yes, infliction is essentially synonymous with cause.

E. No, only a wound can be inflicted.

QUESTION 5

A man is being arrested by a police officer and she is restraining him. The man wriggles to escape from the police officer's grasp and they both topple over. The police officer falls to the floor with the man on top of her, splitting her head open and suffering a serious concussion. The man did not intend, nor did he foresee any risk, that the police officer would suffer any harm as a result of his attempt to break free from her restraint. The man was immediately picked up by a fellow police officer and charged with s 18 OAPA 1861, in that he had maliciously caused GBH while intending to resist arrest. The man asserts the mens rea of the offence has not been made out.

Is the man correct?

A. Yes, the man must successfully resist arrest for the offence to be satisfied.

B. Yes, although the man intended to resist arrest, he must also be malicious as to the causing of harm.

C. No, the man need only intend to resist arrest for the offence to be satisfied.

D. No, the man need only intend to resist arrest and cause GBH for the offence to be made out.

E. Yes, the man must intend to resist arrest and intend to cause GBH.

■ ANSWERS TO QUESTIONS

Answers to 'What do you know already?' questions at the start of the chapter

1) The defendant must cause another person to apprehend the application of immediate unlawful violence.

2) False. There is no requirement that injury should be suffered for a battery to be made out. Indeed, if harm results from a battery you should be looking to the statutory offences.

3) The mens rea for assault occasioning ABH is the same as assault and battery. The mens rea of a s 47 offence is unusual as it only sits within the base offence. You need only establish whether the defendant intended or was subjectively reckless as to application of force or causing the victim to apprehend application of immediate force. There is no additional mens rea requirement in relation to the harm.

4) The mens rea of a s 20 offence requires that the defendant intends or foresees some harm, they do not have to foresee GBH or a wound.

5) Section 18 is a specific-intent offence. It is an intention-only offence and it has an ulterior intent.

Answers to end-of-chapter SQE1-style questions

Question 1:
   The correct answer was E. An assault can be committed by silence (so option A is wrong) and by someone who is not proximate to the victim. However, there must be an expectation of, at least, an imminent application of unlawful force (so option D is wrong) and on the facts this is not satisfied. Option B is incorrect because it fails to sufficiently describe the requirement of immediacy. Option C is incorrect as an assault does not require any use of force; the appropriate offence there would be battery.

Question 2:
   The correct answer was C. A battery is merely the application of unlawful force and there is no requirement that the victim anticipates that force (ie that an assault precedes a battery – so option A is wrong), nor that it results in any harm (so option B is wrong). Option D is wrong because it incorrectly describes the offence of battery and option E is incorrect as the woman has not sustained any injury, therefore an offence contrary to s 47 could not be made out.

Question 3:
   The correct answer was B. There is no mens rea in relation to the causing of ABH. The only mens rea required is that for the assault or, as in this case, the battery. As all other options refer to some requirement of mens rea in respect of injury, they are all incorrect.

Question 4:
   The correct answer was D. Infliction is now understood to be essentially synonymous with cause. All other options suggest different interpretations of the word 'infliction', all of which are not an accurate reflection of the law.

Question 5:

The correct answer was B. A s 18 offence not only requires that the ulterior intent is satisfied, here the intention to resist arrest, but also that the man intends or is subjectively reckless as to harm, probably serious harm (so option C is wrong). Option A is wrong because there is no requirement in law for the man to successfully resist arrest. Option D is wrong because there is an additional requirement of maliciousness when a man is alleged to have resisted lawful apprehension. Option E is wrong because the requirement is that the man either intends or is reckless as to causing harm; there is no requirement of intention alone.

■ KEY CASES, RULES, STATUTES AND INSTRUMENTS

The SQE1 Assessment Specification does not require you to know any case names for the topic of non-fatal offences against the person. It has identified, however, that candidates must know ss 47, 20 and 18 of the OAPA 1861.

7

Theft offences

■ MAKE SURE YOU KNOW

This chapter will cover the core principles of criminal liability for what the Solicitors Regulation Authority (SRA) refer to as 'theft offences'. For the purposes of SQE1, 'theft offences' refer to: theft, robbery, burglary and aggravated burglary. You are required to know each offence in turn, and be able to identify and apply the relevant law appropriately and effectively to realistic client-based problems and situations.

The SQE1 Assessment Specification has not identified that candidates are required to recall/recite any case names for the topic of theft offences. It does identify, however, that candidates must know ss 1, 8, 9 and 10 of the Theft Act (TA) 1968. It is likely that a multiple-choice question (MCQ) may be asked making direct reference to the statutory number, as opposed to the name of the offence itself. For example, it is likely that you may be asked whether a 's 8 offence has been committed', as opposed to whether 'an offence of robbery has been committed'.

'Theft Offences' What they are and how to distinguish them	

Theft (TA 1968, s 1) Stealing property from another	**Burglary (TA 1968, s 9)** Trespassing in a building and intending to commit/committing/attempting to commit an offence
Robbery (TA 1968, s 8) Stealing property from another AND using force or fear of force in order to steal	**Aggravated Burglary (TA 1968, s 10)** Trespassing in a building and intending to commit/committing/attempting to commit an offence AND having an aggravating article at the point of doing so

Overview of theft offences

■ SQE ASSESSMENT ADVICE

As you work through this chapter, remember to pay particular attention in your revision to:
- the distinction between the offences of theft, robbery, burglary and aggravated burglary, and how the choice of offence is determined
- the commonalities between the offences and the fundamental themes shared by the offences
- the actus reus and mens rea requirements of each offence, and how each element can be proven.

■ WHAT DO YOU KNOW ALREADY?

Have a go at these questions before reading this chapter. If you find some difficult or cannot remember the answers, make a note to look more closely at that area during your revision.

1) Fill in the blank: it is possible for land to be stolen in three circumstances; these are _____.

   [Theft, pages 151–163]

2) True or false: a defendant who uses force in order to escape having stolen property from a jewellery store can be liable for robbery.

   [Robbery, pages 163–167]

3) Identify the differences between a s 9(1)(a) burglary, and a s 9(1)(b) burglary in respect of the ulterior offences.

   [Burglary, pages 167–172]

4) Fill in the blank: aggravated burglary requires the defendant to have with him, at the point of committing a burglary, an aggravating article. An aggravating article includes _____.

   [Aggravated burglary, pages 172–175]

INTRODUCING THEFT OFFENCES

The TA 1968 is the primary authority relevant to theft-type offences. While the TA 1968 deals with a variety of offences, the SQE1 Assessment Specification has identified four offences that you need to be prepared to deal with in SQE1. These offences are:

• theft (TA 1968, s 1)
• robbery (TA 1968, s 8)
• burglary (TA 1968, s 9)
• aggravated burglary (TA 1968, s 10).

These offences share many characteristics, such as the notion of property and dishonesty, and are largely interrelated. For example, a robbery cannot be committed unless a theft has been committed. Despite these similarities and elements of cross-over, each offence will be considered separately.

THEFT

The offence of theft in s 1 TA 1968 can be broken down into the five elements detailed in **Figure 7.1**.

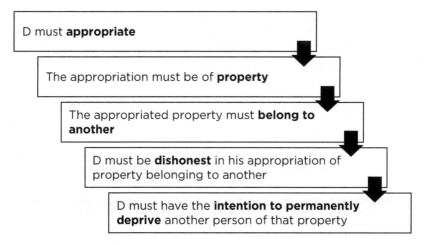

Figure 7.1: Elements of theft

Appropriation

The first requirement is that a defendant must appropriate property. The meaning of **appropriation** is dealt with in s 3 of the TA 1968.

Key term: appropriation

'Appropriation' is concerned with dealing with property as though you are the owner. Such dealings may include:
- gifting the property to another
- selling the property
- damaging or destroying the property, etc.

The offence of theft is so widely drawn that merely touching the property is sufficient to amount to an appropriation. There are a number of questions we need to ask in order to understand the full extent of appropriation.

How many 'rights' must someone appropriate?

An owner of property will possess a number of rights in relation to property (often referred to as a 'bundle of rights'). For theft, it is sufficient if only one of these rights has been appropriated.

Does an appropriation require physical touching?

There is no need for a 'physical' appropriation. It is possible to appropriate property in circumstances where the defendant never lays a hand on the property; so long as their conduct falls within the remit of the rights of the owner. In *R v Pitham* (1977) 65 Cr App R 45, an invitation to purchase the victim's furniture was equivalent to appropriation – even though there was no touching of the property concerned.

Can someone appropriate even though they have been given permission?

The offence of theft requires no 'adverse interference' with the rights of another, meaning that you can appropriate property even where another person has consented to you doing so (see **Practice example 7.1**).

Practice example 7.1

Edwin sold electrical goods to his friends, who bought them through the use of two building society cheques. Edwin was aware that the cheques were stolen. Edwin obtained the consent of the store manager to allow the sale, though he did not inform the manager that the cheques were stolen.

Has Edwin appropriated property in this instance?

> These were the facts of *DPP v Gomez* [1993] AC 442. The House of Lords held that Edwin had appropriated the electrical goods even though he had the consent of the store manager to sell them. His permission to do so was irrelevant; there was still an appropriation.

The principle in *Gomez* extends to situations where the defendant has received property as a gift from another (*R v Hinks* [2001] 2 AC 241).

Can someone appropriate something that they have found and kept?

The wording of s 3(1) is broad enough to deal with the situation in which a defendant comes about the property lawfully but then decides to keep it. Section 3(1) is clear that a defendant can appropriate property by 'keeping or dealing with it as owner'. This is often referred to as a 'secondary' or 'later' appropriation.

For example, suppose that Sam goes to a friend's house for a party, taking her overcoat with her. Upon leaving, she picks up what she mistakenly believes to be her overcoat, but in fact the coat belongs to her friend. Sam only realises this when she gets home but decides to keep it. In this example, Sam will have appropriated the coat. If the other elements of the offence are made out, she will be liable for theft at the point that she possessed the dishonest intention to keep the coat.

Can someone appropriate something that they have lawfully paid for?

What is the situation where a party lawfully obtains property by purchasing it, in circumstances when they did not know that the property was originally stolen? This is often referred to as the 'bona fide purchaser' defence and is prescribed in s 3(2) of the TA 1968. The bona fide purchaser is an innocent third party that has come across the stolen property after lawfully purchasing it (ie paying for it or giving something of value in return) where they had no knowledge that the property was stolen. In this situation, the bona fide purchaser will not be considered as appropriating the property given that the property lawfully belongs to them.

For example, Mark visits his local car salesman to find a bargain car he can use as a 'runaround'. He spots a car valued at what he thinks is a 'pretty reasonable price for its age' and purchases it on the spot with cash. It turns out that the car was stolen, however Mark had no knowledge of this. In this example, Mark has not appropriated property given that he has come across it honestly (ie in bona fide) and for value.

Property

The second element of the offence is that what is appropriated amounts to **property**.

Key term: property

'Property' includes money and all other property, real or personal, including things in action and other intangible property (TA 1968, s 4(1)).

We can summarise the key words from s 4(1) here:

* *'Money'*: means coins or banknotes of any currency.
* *'Real' property*: means land (also known as 'realty'). 'Land' includes the ground itself and anything attached to it (eg a house). As we will see in **Table 7.1**, in general a person cannot steal land, except in a number of small circumstances.
* *'Personal' property*: means anything that is not land (ie is not real property). Personal property is also referred to as 'personalty' and can be classified as follows:
   - *Things (or 'choses') in possession*: tangible property that can be touched and moved, for example a watch, smartphone or a car.
   - *Things (or 'choses') in action*: intangible property such as a bank account, cheque or intellectual property.

For a greater discussion as to what does, and does not, amount to 'land', see *Revise SQE Land Law*.

Theft of land

Land cannot generally be stolen (TA 1968, s 4(2)). There are, however, a number of exceptions to this rule, as demonstrated in **Table 7.1**.

Furthermore, s 4(3) provides that no offence of theft is committed where an individual 'picks' mushrooms, or flowers, fruit or foliage from a plant *unless* they do so for a reward, for sale or for any other commercial purpose. What does this mean in practice?

* Mark trespassing on Sam's land and picking a flower head from a shrub will commit no offence if he gives the flower to Adam as a gift (though he may be liable for criminal damage – see **Chapter 9**).
* Mark will commit an offence, however, if he picks flowers to sell them at his flower stall in the local market.

Importantly, s 4(3) only relates to the 'picking' of certain flora; an offence is still committed if a defendant uproots or removes an entire plant belonging to another (regardless of any commercial purpose) (see **Table 7.1**).

Table 7.1: Theft of land

Explanation and examples
Land may be stolen in circumstances where an individual is entrusted with the land, for example: • a trustee • a personal representative • a person authorised with power of attorney (not merely someone who purports or holds themselves out as being authorised). For example, a trustee selling land belonging to a trust, in breach of trust.
Any person can steal from land if they appropriate something that forms part of the land by severing it, causing it to be severed or appropriating after it has been severed. For example, a neighbour cutting down a tree branch that is encroaching on their land commits theft by severing the branch from the tree.
A tenant may be guilty of theft if he appropriates a fixture, or part of a fixture or structure, that forms part of the land. For example, a tenant is guilty of theft if he appropriates a kitchen cupboard.

Theft of things in action

A thing in action is an intangible right allowing someone to enforce a right against another in law (eg suing an individual for a debt owed is a thing in action). Such rights amount to property that can be stolen and include:

• *Bank accounts*: suppose Mark logs into Sam's online banking and transfers £1,000 from her account to his own personal account. Mark has appropriated Sam's right to control the money in her account.
• *Cheques*: suppose that in retaliation, Sam draws a cheque using Mark's chequebook and forges his signature. Should Sam present that cheque at her bank, to credit her own account, she will have appropriated Mark's right to control the money in his account.

Theft of other property

Remember, s 4(1) uses the phrase 'all other property'. **Table 7.2** (overleaf) deals with some examples of 'other property' that have arisen in the case law.

Belonging to another

The third and final element of the actus reus of the offence is that the property, which has been appropriated, must **belong to another**.

Table 7.2: Theft of other property

Property	Explanation
Animals	Tamed animals, such as pets or animals in a zoo, can be stolen. The position of wild (untamed) animals is somewhat more complex. A wild creature can amount to 'property' if it has been, or is in the process of being, 'reduced into possession'.
Electricity, gas and water	Electricity cannot be stolen. Gas and water, on the other hand, can be stolen if, for example, it is siphoned from a container.
Confidential information	Confidential information is not 'property' that can be stolen (*Oxford v Moss* (1978) 68 Cr App R 183 – it is not theft to copy questions from an examination paper). Had D taken the exam paper, this could have been theft of the paper.
Human bodies and other bodily matters	Human bodies and body parts cannot be generally stolen unless 'they have acquired different attributes by virtue of the application of skill, such as dissection or preservation techniques, for exhibition or teaching purposes' (*R v Kelly; R v Lindsay* [1999] QB 621, per Rose LJ). Bodily fluids such as semen and urine are classed as property and can be stolen (eg a urine sample stolen from police evidence).
Services	Services do not constitute 'property' and cannot be stolen – though separate offences of making off without payment and fraud will cover this gap in the law.
Unlawful property	Illegal or unlawful property can be stolen. For example, D can steal property that has already been stolen, and can steal property that is unlawful (eg stealing drugs from a drug dealer).

Key term: belonging to another

Property will belong to another person where they have possession or control over it or any proprietary right or interest in it (TA 1968, s 5(1)).

Ownership of the property is not a requirement; a theft may occur where property is appropriated from an individual who is merely borrowing the item in question. A court may find that property belongs to another where, for example, another person:

• owns the property

- has physical possession over the property
- has a lien, or some other form of security over the property.

Given the irrelevance of ownership to 'belonging to another', it is possible for a defendant to steal his own property (see **Practice example 7.2**).

Practice example 7.2
Frank takes his car to a local garage to be repaired. Frank states that he will pay for the repairs and take the car away the next day. Instead, and at night, Frank takes the car from the garage having not paid for the repairs. Does the car 'belong to another'? **These were the facts of *R v Turner (No 2)* [1971] 2 All ER 441. The Court of Appeal ruled that the car 'belonged' to the garage in that they held possession and control over the car, until Frank had paid for the repairs, at the time it was taken by Frank.**

Section 5 goes on to identify further circumstances in which property will belong to another. **Table 7.3** deals with these circumstances.

Table 7.3: Belonging to another in s 5

Explanation and examples
Assets that form part of the trust fund will amount to 'property' within s 4. Given the nature of fragmentation of title in a trust, the trust property belongs to both the trustee of a trust (who possesses legal title) and the beneficiary of a trust (who possesses equitable title). In that regard, the property belongs to both the trustee and beneficiary, and there can be an appropriation by either party against the rights of the other.
If money is given to D with an obligation that it is used for a particular purpose, the property is treated as belonging to another. If D fails to use it for that purpose, he may be liable for theft. For example, in *R v Wain* [1995] 2 Cr App R 660, D was in possession of money raised for a charity. Instead of using the money as intended (for the charity), D spent the money for his own purposes and was guilty of theft.
If money is given to D by mistake, and there is an obligation to correct that mistake, the property will continue to belong to another. If D fails to restore any property received in mistake, he is liable for theft. For example, in *AG's Reference (No 1 of 1983)* [1985] QB 182, D had been credited for a shift that she had not worked. The money paid still belonged to her employer as a result of the mistake, and thus D was liable for theft by her failure to rectify the mistake.

Where property has been abandoned (in the sense that the owner has relinquished their rights over it), it cannot thereafter be stolen. Do not confuse, however, circumstances where property is abandoned from other similar circumstances:

- Where property is merely lost, and not abandoned, it can still be stolen.
- Where property is donated to a charity shop, it will not be abandoned (and can thus be stolen) if it is simply left outside of the shop waiting to be picked up by the charity workers.
- Where property is thrown away (in a dustbin, for example), it can still be stolen on account that the owner has chosen to allow refuse collectors to take property away and destroy it.

Dishonesty

The first element of the mens rea is that the defendant is dishonest in his appropriation of property belonging to another. The majority of theft cases turn on whether the prosecution can prove the defendant's **dishonesty**.

Key term: dishonesty

The TA 1968 does not define the term 'dishonesty'. Dishonesty is assessed objectively by asking whether D is dishonest in his conduct according to the standards of ordinary decent people.

When dealing with dishonesty, you should first deal with s 2(1) TA 1968, before then dealing with the common law test for dishonesty.

TA 1968, s 2(1)

The TA 1968 identifies three circumstances in which a person's appropriation of property belonging to another is *not* to be regarded as dishonest. These circumstances (often referred to as 'honest appropriations') are contained in s 2(1) and are explained in **Table 7.4** (overleaf). In all of these circumstances, the defendant's belief does *not* need to be reasonably held, but must be honest (though, the more unreasonable a belief, the more likely it was not genuinely held).

In addition to the above, s 2(2) TA 1968 makes it clear that appropriation of property may still be considered dishonest where the defendant is willing to pay for the property. A willingness to pay will be considered under the common law test for dishonesty.

Table 7.4: Honest appropriations

Explanation and examples
If D holds a genuine belief that he has a right in law to deprive another person of property, he will not be dishonest in his appropriation. The right in law may be for himself, or on behalf of another person. For example, in *R v Robinson* [1977] Crim LR 173, D was owed money by V. During a fight, D forcibly took the money owed from V. D was not liable for robbery on the basis that he believed that he had a right in law to the money owed.
If D holds a genuine, albeit mistaken, belief that he would have consent to appropriate the property, had the party who could provide consent known of the appropriation and the circumstances, he will not be dishonest in his appropriation. For example, Mark and Sam share an apartment together. Mark drinks Sam's wine genuinely believing that she would consent to him doing so. Mark, in this case, will not be liable for theft.
If D holds a genuine belief that the person to whom the property belongs to cannot be discovered by taking reasonable steps, he will not be dishonest in his appropriation. Reference to 'reasonable' concerns the steps to be taken to discover the person to whom the property belongs. For example, in *R v Small* (1988) 86 Cr App R 170, D was not liable for theft having taken a car that he genuinely believed to be abandoned.

Common law test for dishonesty

Should the circumstances in s 2(1) not apply, a court would then determine whether a defendant is dishonest according to the common law test.

The common law test is that stated in the cases of *Ivey v Genting Casinos (UK) Ltd t/a (Crockfords)* [2017] UKSC 67 and *R v Barton; R v Booth* [2020] EWCA Crim 575. You are not required to know these cases for the purposes of SQE1, but must understand the principles from them. The test can be laid out in **Figure 7.2** (overleaf).

In respect of the defendant's subjective beliefs (stage 1 of *Ivey*):
• Reference to 'as to the facts' means taking account of the defendant's state of knowledge. This includes everything that has led 'an accused to act as he or she did'. The experience and intelligence of the accused in forming his belief should also be considered, where relevant (*R v Barton; R v Booth*, per Lord Burnett CJ).
• The state of belief on the part of the defendant need not be reasonably held, but must be genuinely held (reasonableness will be a relevant factor, however, as to whether the belief was genuinely held).

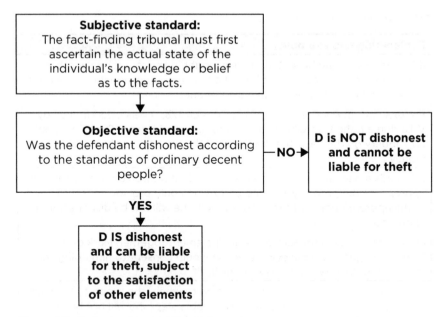

Figure 7.2: Common law test for dishonesty

In respect of the objective evaluation by the arbiters of fact (stage 2 of *Ivey*):
• There is no requirement that the defendant must subjectively appreciate that what he has done is, by those standards, dishonest.

Intention to permanently deprive

The final requirement for the offence of theft to be made out is that the defendant must intend, by his appropriation, to permanently deprive another of his property. The words **intention to permanently deprive** should be afforded their ordinary meaning.

> ### Key term: intention to permanently deprive
>
> • *Intention*: there is no requirement for D to succeed in permanently depriving another of the property; an intention is sufficient. The offence is one of specific intent.
> • *Permanently*: a temporary deprivation is not sufficient (though see s 6 below).
> • *Deprive*: the intention must be to deprive another of the property; it is irrelevant whether D intends to make a gain for himself (compare with fraud in **Chapter 8**).

In the majority of cases, whether such an intention is made out will be obvious. In the minority of cases, however, the defendant's intention to permanently deprive is not so obvious. In these exceptional cases, assistance may be gleaned from s 6 TA 1968. The wording of the statute itself is complex and **Table 7.5** highlights the key features of s 6.

Table 7.5: Intention to permanently deprive and s 6

General premise	Explanation and examples
Where D's intention is to treat the property as his own to deal with regardless of another's rights (TA 1968, s 6(1))	• If D intends to treat property as his own, though not meaning the other person to lose the property itself, this can still be treated as an intention to permanently deprive. In *R v Marshall* [1998] 2 Cr App R 282, D sold on used, but unexpired, London Underground tickets and travel cards. While the tickets were eventually returned to London Underground, D had treated the tickets as his own, disregarding the rights of London Underground. • An intention to treat things as one's own can also be seen in cases where property is ransomed (ie will only be returned to the owner upon satisfaction of a condition), or where property is replaced (eg taking money from a till and replacing it the next week). • Borrowing and lending may also amount to an intention to permanently deprive in cases where the borrowing is equivalent to an outright taking or disposal. A borrowing has such equivalence where the value or virtue of the property is lost or reduced when it is returned (eg Sam borrows Mark's theatre tickets without his consent, watches the show and then returns the tickets; in this case, the tickets are now worthless).
Where D parts with the property at the risk of non-return (TA 1968, s 6(2))	If D parts with the property appropriated, and there is a risk that he will not get that property back, he will be treated as having an intention to permanently deprive. For example, suppose Mark takes Sam's silver earrings and pawns them for £500 in order to pay off some of his debts. In this scenario, while Mark is capable of retrieving the property (by redeeming it), there is a risk that he will not be able to do so. Therefore, Mark would be held as having an intention to permanently deprive.

A defendant may also be liable for theft where they merely hold a conditional intention to steal (ie an intention to steal only if there is something of value to the defendant worth stealing).

Summary: what do we know about theft?	
What does 'appropriation' mean?	Appropriation refers to the assumption of the rights of another. D can appropriate even if they have consent, and need only appropriate one of the rights of another.
What is the meaning of 'property'?	Property refers to money or any other types of property, whether real or personal. Land cannot generally be stolen, unless a circumstance in s 4(2) applies.
When does property 'belong to another'?	Property will belong to another where another person has possession, control or a proprietary interest in that property. Property will continue to belong to another if it is received for a particular purpose or by mistake.
What is the meaning of 'dishonesty'?	Dishonesty is not defined in the TA 1968. First, the court will consider whether D was 'honest' in his appropriation, by use of the circumstances in s 2(1) TA 1968. The court may then consider the common law test for dishonesty, which asks whether D was objectively dishonest according to the standards of ordinary decent people. In order to answer this question, the arbiters of fact will first identify the subjective state of knowledge or belief held by D. Whether D appreciates that his conduct was dishonest is irrelevant.
What is the requirement that D must have the 'intention to permanently deprive'?	Intention to permanently deprive should be afforded its ordinary meaning. In most cases, an intention will be obvious. Where it is not so clear, the court may consider s 6 TA 1968, and identify whether D's dealing with the property could be considered as being equivalent to an outright taking.

ROBBERY

The offence of robbery in s 8 TA 1968 can be broken down into five elements (see **Figure 7.3**).

We shall deal with each element in turn below.

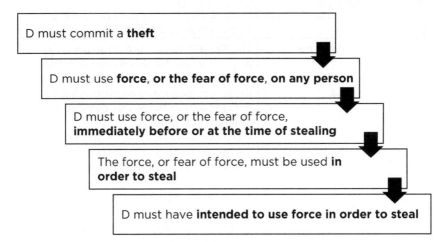

Figure 7.3: Elements of robbery

Theft

The first requirement is fairly self-explanatory: the defendant must commit a theft. This requirement exists on account that robbery is, in essence, an aggravated form of theft.

Therefore, in order for a robbery to be charged, one must first prove all five elements of theft dealt with in **Figure 7.1**. If any of the elements of theft are missing, the defendant cannot be liable for robbery.

Force or fear of force on any person

The second requirement is that the defendant must *either*:
• use force on any person, or
• put or seek to put any person in fear of being then and there subjected to force.

Use of force

The TA 1968 does not define the words 'uses force on any person'. 'Force' is an ordinary English word and it is for the jury to determine, as a matter of fact, whether the defendant has used force on another person.

There are two fundamental principles that come with this requirement, and these are set out in **Table 7.6**.

Table 7.6: Principles of 'uses force on any person'

Principle	Explanation and examples
Force used need not be substantial	The TA 1968 requires that force is used on any person; there is no requirement that the force be substantial. It is for the jury to determine whether what D did amounts to force. This can lead to different outcomes: • *R v Dawson* (1977) 64 Cr App R 170: jostling a man and causing him to lose his balance could be sufficient to amount to robbery. • *R v Clouden* [1987] Crim LR 56: wrenching a shopping basket from the hands of the victim amounted to the use of 'force' for the purposes of robbery.
Force used need not be directly applied to the victim	Force can be applied indirectly in circumstances where, for example, the force is directed at the property as opposed to the person (eg by snatching a handbag or handbasket from the victim, as in *R v Clouden*).

Fear of force

The alternative actus reus here is that the defendant 'puts or seeks to put any person in fear of being then and there subjected to force'. Reference to the word 'fear' does not mean that the victim must be 'afraid'. Rather, the word 'fear' is used to mean that the victim must 'apprehend' that force will be used (similar to assault, as considered in **Chapter 6**).

Fear of force may be satisfied in two ways, as illustrated in **Figure 7.4** (overleaf).

Furthermore, the fear must be that force will be applied 'then and there'. In essence, the victim must apprehend the use of force in the immediate future.

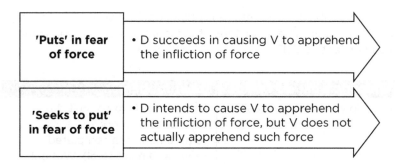

| **'Puts' in fear of force** | • D succeeds in causing V to apprehend the infliction of force |

| **'Seeks to put' in fear of force** | • D intends to cause V to apprehend the infliction of force, but V does not actually apprehend such force |

Figure 7.4: Fear of force in robbery

On any person
Force, or the fear of force, must be used on 'any person'. Force or fear of force need not be used on the person to whom the property belongs; it may be used on a different person.

Immediately before or at the time of stealing
The force, or fear of force, must be used on any person 'immediately before or at the time' of stealing.

In order to steal
The fourth requirement is that the force, or the fear of force, must be used 'in order to steal'. 'In order to steal' simply means that the force is used to enable the theft to take place and is a matter to be determined by the jury. Please note the following two points:
- Where force is used *in order to escape* but not in order to steal, there will be no robbery. For example, Mark pushes a security guard out of the way in order to escape with a watch stolen from the jewellery shop counter.
- Where theft is merely an *afterthought* to the use of force, there will be no robbery. For example, suppose that Mark and Sam get into a fist fight because they do not like each other. Sam knocks Mark to the floor and decides, while Mark is unconscious, to steal his wallet. In this example, Sam has not used force in order to steal; the theft appears to be no more than an afterthought.

Intention to use force
Finally, the defendant must intend to use force, or the fear of force, in order to steal. This is a fairly simple requirement looking towards the

defendant's subjective intentions in respect of his conduct. For example, did the defendant intend to cause the victim to fear the application of force in order to steal?

Summary: what do we know about robbery?	
What do we mean by 'steal'?	In order for D to commit the offence of robbery, there is a requirement of a completed theft (ie D must steal). Without a completed theft, there is no offence of robbery.
What is the requirement for D to use 'force' or the 'fear of force'?	D must either use force on any person, in the sense of using force against that person, or he must put, or seek to put, a person in fear of being subjected to force. It is irrelevant whether an individual is put in fear of being subjected to force – it is sufficient that D *seeks to put* the victim in fear of such force.
What does it mean to say that force must be used on 'any person'?	D may use force on any person in order to effect the theft. The force need not be used on the person whom D is stealing from.
What is the meaning of 'immediately before, or at the time of doing so'?	D must use force, or the fear of force, immediately before the dishonest appropriation of property belonging to another, or at the time of the dishonest appropriation.
What is the requirement that force must be used 'in order to steal'?	D must use force, or the fear of force, in order to enable his theft to take place. Should D use force for some purpose other than to steal, or use force in order to escape, there is no liability for robbery.
What must D 'intend' for the offence of robbery?	D must intend to use force, or the fear of force, in order to steal. His intention must be clearly for that purpose.

BURGLARY

The offence of burglary is concerned with criminal trespass and is charged contrary to s 9 TA 1968. Burglary can be committed in two separate ways, listed in s 9(1)(a) and 9(1)(b). Each offence has been broken down in **Table 7.7.**

Table 7.7: Elements of burglary

s 9(1)(a) Burglary	s 9(1)(b) Burglary
(a) D must *enter* a building.	(a) D must have *entered* a building.
(b) The entry must be of a *building or part of a building.*	(b) The entry must be of a *building or part of a building.*
(c) D must be a *trespasser* when he enters the building or part of a building.	(c) D must be a *trespasser* when he enters the building or part of a building.
(d) D must have the necessary *intention or recklessness* as to being a *trespasser.*	(d) D must have the necessary *intention or recklessness* as to being a *trespasser.*
(e) D must *intend to commit one of the ulterior offences.*	(e) D must *commit one of the ulterior offences.*

As you can see, the offences contain a number of similarities, which will be addressed together. There are some key differences between the offences, which are worth highlighting at this point (see **Table 7.8** overleaf).

We can now consider the elements of s 9(1)(a) and 9(1)(b).

Entry

Both s 9(1)(a) and 9(1)(b) require the defendant to enter a building (though they differ in how that requirement is expressed). 'Entry' is not defined in the TA 1968; however, it has been understood by the case law that an entry must be 'effective'. Whether the entry has been effective is a question of fact for the jury. We can identify some principles to assist with understanding 'effective entry':

• *Entry need not be 'substantial'.* This means that the defendant need not have wholly entered the building or part of a building. It is sufficient if only part of the defendant's body is in the building.
• *The defendant need not be 'in a position to' steal, inflict GBH or cause criminal damage.* It is irrelevant that he is not actually able to commit an ulterior offence because, for example, his body gets stuck when he enters the building.

Table 7.8: Distinguishing features of s 9(1)(a) and 9(1)(b)

Distinguishing feature	TA 1968, s 9(1)(a)	TA 1968, s 9(1)(b)
The point at which the offence is committed	At the point of entry, provided that D is a trespasser and possesses the necessary mens rea.	The point at which the ulterior offence is committed; D having already entered the building.
What are the relevant ulterior offences?	(a) stealing anything in the building or part of the building (ie theft) (b) inflicting grievous bodily harm (GBH) on any person therein (c) causing unlawful damage to the building or anything therein (ie criminal damage).	(a) stealing, or attempting to steal, anything in the building or part of the building (ie theft) (b) inflicting, or attempting to inflict, GBH on any person therein.
What must D do re these ulterior offences?	D must merely *intend* to commit one of the ulterior offences; D need not actually commit the offence.	D must commit, or attempt to commit, one of the ulterior offences. A mere intention is insufficient.

- *Entry may be effective by use of an instrument.* For example, the defendant's entry may be effective where he uses an instrument or tool to enable him to steal.
- *Entry may be effective by use of an innocent agent.* For example, the defendant's entry may be effective where he uses an innocent agent (eg a child or someone who lacks mens rea) in order to steal.

Exam warning

Be wary that not all entries will result in a charge or conviction for burglary; whether an entry is effective will depend on the circumstances of the case and the particular degree of entry. An MCQ may seek you to advise whether an entry is 'effective' or not. Entry is likely to be ineffective where it cannot be said on any logical basis that D has 'entered' a building, for example where D sticks his fingers through the letterbox. Think practically about the meaning of 'entry'.

Building or part of a building

The defendant must enter a 'building or part of a building'. This is not restricted to domestic buildings (ie dwellings), but is capable of extending to any structure. The offence of burglary may be committed by trespass into either a building or part of a building.

Building

While the TA 1968 does not define 'building', the common law has identified that a 'building' is an ordinary word and it is a matter of 'fact and degree' as to whether a structure amounts to a building. Some examples of buildings include:

- dwellings
- garden sheds or outhouses
- modular buildings
- caravans or houseboats (if inhabited).

Part of a building

Reference to 'part of a building' is designed to cover the circumstances where the defendant is lawfully within a building but then exceeds their permissions to enter another part of the building (see **Practice example 7.3**).

Practice example 7.3

Terence is found in a department store shortly before closing time. He lawfully entered the store during opening hours. He is observed by a store detective moving behind the counter and opening a till drawer.

Do you think 'behind the counter' amounts to 'part of a building' for the purposes of burglary?

These were the facts of *R v Walkington* [1979] 2 All ER 716. The area behind the counter was restricted to the general public and thus it was open to the jury to find that Terence had trespassed in part of a building.

In essence, you must be able to identify whether the defendant was a trespasser at the original point of entry, or when he moved to a part of the building that was allegedly restricted or closed off to him.

As a trespasser

The defendant must enter, or have entered, a building or part of a building 'as a trespasser'. In the majority of cases, there will be little difficulty in proving that an individual is a trespasser: they likely do not have permission to be in a particular place, at a particular time.

However, there may be circumstances in which it is more difficult to prove that an individual is a trespasser (eg where the defendant claims to have permission to be in a particular location). In these circumstances, a jury would have to look at the alleged permissions granted and whether they prevent the defendant from being classified as a trespasser. For example:

- *Permission may be granted through mistake.* In circumstances where permission to enter has been granted, but that permission is mistaken due to fraud, deception or misinformation, the defendant will be treated as a trespasser.
- *The defendant goes beyond permission granted.* In some circumstances, the defendant may go beyond the permissions granted to him to be in a particular location. In these circumstances, the defendant will be treated as a trespasser.

In addition to the above examples, a defendant may be considered a trespasser in circumstances where permission is withdrawn (though note the **Exam warning** below).

Exam warning

Make sure that you do not overlook the requirement that D is a trespasser, and that you do not confuse the court's position on this. Remember, D must be a trespasser *at the point of entry.* Therefore, if D has lawfully entered a building or part of a building, but then goes on to commit a theft therein, this does not amount to burglary. Instead, this should be charged as simple theft. In the case of withdrawn permission, an individual will only become a trespasser for the purposes of burglary if they, for example, refuse to leave and instead move to a different part of the building (thus entering that part of the building as a trespasser).

Intention or recklessness to enter as a trespasser

Not only must the defendant be a trespasser *in fact*, they must also:

- know that they are entering as a trespasser, and thus enter intentionally as a trespasser, or
- be reckless as to whether or not they are a trespasser.

In both cases, the defendant must intend to be a trespasser, or be reckless as to such, *at the point of entry.*

Revision tip

When considering whether D intended to trespass, or was reckless as to such, pay careful attention to the facts of the case before you. Was force used to gain entry to the building? Has entry been made at an unusual time (eg when a shop is closed)? Are there signs indicating that a particular part of the building is off limits to D? Was D already barred from that particular building? By maintaining a practical focus, you will be able to identify whether D has the necessary mens rea in respect of being a trespasser.

If a defendant holds an honest but mistaken belief that he has permission to enter, then he cannot be liable for burglary. Such belief need not be reasonable; though the more unreasonable a belief is, the less likely it is genuinely held.

Commission of, or intention to commit, an offence while in the building

The final requirement for burglary is dependent on the type of burglary that is alleged (ie s 9(1)(a) or 9(1)(b)). Go back to **Table 7.8** for the distinguishing features.

Some points should be noted:
• For a s 9(1)(a) offence, the defendant must possess the necessary intention *at the point of entry.* An intention *before* or *after* entry is not sufficient.
• It is irrelevant whether the defendant's intention is conditional (eg he will only steal if there is something of value worth stealing). A defendant still has the intention to steal at the point of entry.
• The defendant must either intend to steal, damage property or cause GBH 'therein' the building or actually do so therein. For example, if the defendant carries the householder out of the house and then viciously attacks them, this is unlikely to amount to burglary.
• For a s 9(1)(b) offence, commission of criminal damage is not sufficient (though an intention to cause criminal damage at the point of entry will be sufficient for s 9(1)(a)).

Summary: what do we know about burglary?	
When will D have 'entered' a building?	Entry is an ordinary word, requiring some form of 'effective' entry. D need not be wholly within a building or part of a building (part of his body will be sufficient) and D need not be in a position that would allow him to commit an offence.
What is a 'building or part of a building'	A building is an ordinary word referring to a structure with a degree of permanence. Part of a building refers to an area within a building that is restricted and not open to D.
When will D be a 'trespasser'?	A trespasser is an individual who has entered a building or part of a building without permission to do so. Entry as a trespasser must be deliberate and D must know that he is a trespasser, or be reckless as to whether he is or not.
What needs to happen while in the building?	Mere trespass is not sufficient. It must either be proven that, at the point of entry, D intended to steal, do unlawful damage or inflict GBH, or that D, while in the building, committed or attempted to commit theft or GBH.

AGGRAVATED BURGLARY

The offence of aggravated burglary involves the use of an **aggravating article** to commit burglary and is found in s 10 TA 1968.

Key term: aggravating article
An aggravating article includes a weapon, firearm, imitation firearm or explosive used in connection with the burglary.

The offence can be broken down into three elements, which are identified in **Figure 7.5** (overleaf).

Commits a burglary

As the name suggests, the first requirement is to prove that the defendant committed the offence of burglary.

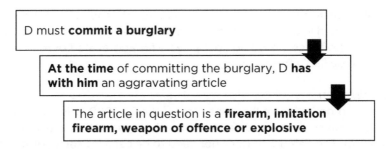

Figure 7.5: Elements of aggravated burglary

At the time he has with him an aggravating article
This particular requirement can be broken down into two elements:
• 'at the time', and
• 'has with him'.

At the time
This requirement is concerned with the point in time at which the defendant must have the aggravating article with him. The appropriate point in time depends on the type of burglary alleged, ie:
• S 9(1)(a): the defendant must have the aggravating article with him *at the point of entry*.
• S 9(1)(b): the defendant must have the aggravating article with him at *the point he steals, or attempts to steal, or inflicts, or attempts to inflict, GBH* (see **Practice example 7.4**).

Practice example 7.4
One evening, Michael forcibly enters a dwelling belonging to a married couple. Michael enters the building unarmed but soon thereafter arms himself with a knife from the kitchen. Michael proceeds up the stairs and confronts the householders, threatening them with the knife and demanding their money and jewellery.

Has Michael committed aggravated burglary?

These were the facts of *R v O'Leary* (1986) 82 Cr App R 341. The Court of Appeal found that while D had entered the dwelling unarmed, the theft took place at the point that D demanded the money and jewellery from the householders. Given that he had the knife with him at that point in time, he was liable for aggravated burglary.

In an alternative circumstance, if, for example, a defendant had entered a building armed with a crowbar but then discarded it prior to committing any ulterior offence, he would not be liable for aggravated burglary (but could still be liable for burglary).

Has with him

There is no definition of 'has with him' in the TA 1968; it is an ordinary phrase meaning that the defendant has the aggravating article within his control. The defendant does not need to be carrying the aggravating article, but must have it readily accessible to him. In addition, the prosecution must prove that the defendant knew that he had the aggravating article in his possession.

Firearm, weapon of offence or explosive

The article being carried by the defendant must either be classed as a firearm, imitation firearm, weapon of offence or explosive. The meaning of these terms can be found in s 10(1)(a)-(c) (and are detailed in **Table 7.9**).

Table 7.9: Offensive articles for use in aggravated burglary

Aggravating article	Explanation
Firearm	Includes an airgun or air pistol.
Imitation firearm	Means anything that has the appearance of being a firearm, whether capable of being discharged or not.
Weapon of offence	Means any article made or adapted for use for causing injury to or incapacitating a person, or intended by the person having it with him for such use. This could include seemingly innocent articles that are used, or intended to be used, for improper purposes. For example, a screwdriver may be used to injure someone, a roll of socks may be used to gag an individual (and thus incapacitate them).
Explosive	Means any article manufactured for the purpose of producing a practical effect by explosion, or intended by the person having it with him for that purpose. A box of matches would not be classed as an explosive.

Revision tip
A common mnemonic that is used, which you may find useful in your revision of the aggravating articles, is 'WIFE':   **w**eapon of offence   **i**mitation firearm   **f**irearm   **e**xplosive.

Summary: what do we know about aggravated burglary?

What does it mean that D must have committed a burglary and 'at the time has with him' an aggravating article?	'At the time' refers to the point in time that the offence is complete. If the prosecution alleges a s 9(1)(a) offence, D must have it with him at the point of entry; and for s 9(1)(b), it must be at the point of committing or attempting to commit theft or GBH.
	'Has with him' refers to D having the article in his possession or having it readily accessible. D must know that he has the article with him.
What are the aggravating articles?	An article may be aggravating if it is a firearm, imitation firearm, weapon of offence or an explosive.

■ KEY POINT CHECKLIST

This chapter has covered the following key knowledge points. You can use these to structure your revision, ensuring you recall the key details for each point, as covered in this chapter.

- Theft is committed where the defendant dishonestly appropriates property belonging to another with the intention to permanently deprive the other of it.
- Robbery occurs where the defendant steals and, immediately before or at the time of doing so, uses force or the fear of force in order to steal.
- Burglary may be committed where the defendant enters a building or part of a building as a trespasser, either with the intention to commit an ulterior offence or where the defendant actually commits an ulterior offence.

- Aggravated burglary occurs where the defendant commits a burglary and, at the point of committing that burglary, he has with him an aggravating article.

■ KEY TERMS AND CONCEPTS

- appropriation (**page 152**)
- property (**page 154**)
- belonging to another (**page 156**)
- dishonesty (**page 158**)
- intention to permanently deprive (**page 160**)
- aggravating article (**page 172**)

■ SQE1-STYLE QUESTIONS

QUESTION 1

A man is invited to his friend's bungalow for a party. While at the party, the man gets into a fight with the friend's brother. The man is asked to leave the house immediately. Upon being asked to leave, the man intends to cause damage to some property in order to teach his friend a lesson. Instead of leaving the house, the man walks into a bedroom and begins to urinate on the furniture, causing irreparable damage.

Is the man guilty of burglary contrary to s 9 Theft Act (TA) 1968?

A. No, the man cannot be guilty of burglary as he was not a trespasser in the bungalow at the point of entry.

B. No, the man cannot be guilty of burglary as the commission of criminal damage is not an offence that can satisfy the offence of burglary under s 9(1)(b) TA 1968.

C. Yes, the man entered the bedroom as a trespasser with the intention to commit criminal damage, which can satisfy the offence of burglary under s 9(1)(a) TA 1968.

D. Yes, the man became a trespasser immediately upon being asked to leave the house and any damage caused thereafter can satisfy the offence of burglary under s 9(1)(b) TA 1968.

E. No, the man cannot be guilty of burglary as he did not intend to cause criminal damage at the point of entry into the bungalow.

QUESTION 2

A husband and wife are walking down the high street when they are approached by a woman. The woman threatens the couple with a knife. The woman points the knife at the husband and demands money from the wife, threatening to stab the husband if she does not hand over the money. Neither of the couple are afraid that force will be used against them but hand over money in order for the woman to leave them alone.

Which of the following best describes the liability of the woman?

A. The woman cannot be liable for robbery because the couple did not fear that they would be subjected to force there and then.

B. The woman cannot be liable for robbery because she did not use actual force on the couple in order to steal.

C. The woman can be liable for robbery because the offence requires the use of a weapon in order to steal.

D. The woman can be liable for robbery because she sought to put the couple in fear of being there and then subjected to force; it was irrelevant that they did not actually fear force.

E. The woman cannot be liable for robbery because force was directed at the husband, but the property was stolen from the wife.

QUESTION 3

Late at night, a man enters, as a trespasser, a home belonging to an elderly couple. At the point of entry, the man is carrying a gun with him. Once inside the house, the man places the gun in his pocket. The man enters the bedroom of the couple and demands their jewellery. When the couple refuse to hand over any jewellery, the man points to his pocket and says, 'I've got a gun, now give me the jewellery.' The couple are terrified at the threat as they can see the outline of the gun through the man's trousers. The couple hand over all of their jewellery. The man is caught as he is escaping the house and it is discovered that the gun was unloaded and thus incapable of firing. The man is charged with aggravated burglary on the basis that he stole jewellery.

Which of the following best describes the liability of the man?

A. The man cannot be liable for aggravated burglary on account that he was not carrying the gun in his hand at the time that he stole the jewellery from the couple.

B. The man can be liable for aggravated burglary because he had the gun with him at the point of stealing the jewellery, and it was immaterial whether the gun was loaded or not.

C. The man cannot be liable for aggravated burglary because the gun was unloaded and incapable of firing.

D. The man can be liable for aggravated burglary because he had the gun in his hand at the point of entry into the house.

E. The man cannot be liable for aggravated burglary because the couple never saw the gun and thus could not have been threatened by the presence of a mere outline in the man's trousers.

QUESTION 4

A man is walking through the park when he notices a cyclist sitting on a bench, with a bicycle propped against the side of the bench. The man sneaks up to the bench and takes the bicycle without the cyclist realising. The man is later apprehended and claims that he believed the bicycle had recently been stolen from his friend and he was merely returning it to his friend. This belief is mistaken and the bicycle did not belong to the man's friend.

Is the man guilty of theft?

A. Yes, the man may be dishonest because the property did not belong to him, and therefore he cannot claim that he has a right in law to appropriate the property.

B. Yes, the man may be dishonest because there is sufficient evidence for the jury to be sure that his belief that the property belongs to his friend is unreasonable.

C. Yes, the man may be dishonest because there is sufficient evidence for the jury to be sure that he appreciated that his conduct was dishonest to the standards of ordinary decent people.

D. Yes, the man may be dishonest because he had no moral right to appropriate the property.

E. Yes, the man may be dishonest because there is sufficient evidence for the jury to be sure that his belief that the property belongs to his friend is not genuinely held.

QUESTION 5

A student enters a school late at night with the intention of copying the answers to the test that he is to sit the next day. The student enters his classroom and finds the test paper in his teacher's desk. The student takes a photograph on his smartphone of the answers. Before leaving the classroom, the student charges his phone, using the plug socket behind his teacher's desk. As the student is about to leave the classroom, he takes a silver pen from his teacher's desk. As the student leaves the building, he picks a number of berries from a bush in the school's garden and eats them.

Which of the following best describes the liability of the student for theft?

A. The student is liable for theft in respect of the pen and the berries, but not liable for theft in respect of the exam answers or charging his phone.

B. The student is liable for theft in respect of the pen, but is not liable for theft in respect of any of the other items listed.

C. The student is not liable for theft in respect of any of the items listed.

D. The student is liable for theft in respect of the pen and the test answers, but is not liable for theft in respect of any of the other items listed.

E. The student is liable for theft in respect of all of the items listed.

■ ANSWERS TO QUESTIONS

Answers to 'What do you know already?' questions at the start of the chapter

1) It is possible for land to be stolen in three circumstances identified in s 4(2) TA 1968.

2) False. To be liable for robbery, the defendant must use force, or the fear of force, 'in order to steal'. Force used to escape is not sufficient for burglary unless it can be said that the theft is continuing at the point such force is used.

3) There are two offences of burglary contained in s 9 TA 1968. Section 9(1)(a) only requires an intention to commit theft, GBH or unlawful damage, while s 9(1)(b) requires that the defendant attempts to commit, or actually commits, an offence of theft or GBH.

4) Aggravated burglary requires the defendant to have with him, at the point of committing a burglary, an aggravating article. An aggravating article includes a weapon of offence, imitation firearm, firearm or explosive (WIFE).

Answers to end-of-chapter SQE1-style questions

Question 1:

The correct answer was C. This is because the man became a trespasser when he moved from one part of the building to another after having his permission revoked by the householder. The man held an intention to commit damage at the point of entry into the bedroom and can be liable for burglary. Option A is incorrect because an individual is capable of entering property lawfully and subsequently becoming a trespasser. While the statement in option B is accurate, in that criminal damage is not an ulterior offence capable of satisfying the offence in s 9(1)(b), the statement is incorrect because the man can be liable for an offence contrary to s 9(1)(a). Option D is wrong on account that the man did not 'enter' as a trespasser until he moved into the bedroom; he must be permitted a reasonable amount of time to leave the bungalow. Furthermore, criminal damage does not satisfy an offence under s 9(1)(b). Option E is incorrect because it is sufficient that the man intends to cause criminal damage at the point of entry into the bedroom.

Question 2:

The correct answer was D. This is because a woman may be liable where they seek to put another person in fear of force, even if that person is not actually fearful of such force (therefore option A is wrong). The use of force is not required; the fear of force is sufficient (so option B is wrong) and there is no requirement for a weapon to be used in a robbery (so option C is incorrect also). Option E is incorrect because robbery requires force to be used on 'any person' and does not require it to be used on the person from whom the property is stolen.

Question 3:

The correct answer was B. This is because the phrase 'has with him' means that the article is under his control, which it would be if it is in his pocket, and does not require that the man is carrying an aggravating article by hand (therefore option A is incorrect). The gun need not be loaded or capable of firing in order to be a firearm (therefore option C is wrong). Option D is incorrect on account that the man is seemingly charged with aggravated burglary using s 9(1)(b). If that is the case, the focus is whether the man had the gun at the time of stealing the jewellery, not at the time of entry. Option E is wrong on account that there is no requirement that the victims see the aggravating article; the focus is on the man's possession or control of it.

Question 4:

The correct answer was E. This is because a claim by the man that he held a mistaken belief that he held a right in law to appropriate the property must be genuinely held. There is sufficient evidence for the jury to conclude that the belief was not genuinely held (eg he could have spoken to the cyclist about his concerns). The belief need not be reasonable, so option B is wrong as it places incorrect emphasis on unreasonableness. Option A is incorrect as the right in law may be on behalf of the man himself, or on behalf of a third party (eg his friend). Option C is wrong as it incorrectly states the common law test for dishonesty, which does not require the man to subjectively appreciate that his conduct is dishonest. Option D is wrong because the focus is on whether the man genuinely held a belief in law, not in morality.

Question 5:

The correct answer was B. This is because the pen is the only piece of property that is capable of being stolen. Berries that are picked from a plant cannot be stolen unless they are picked for reward, sale or any other commercial purpose (therefore options A and E are wrong). Option C is wrong because the pen is personal property that can be stolen. Option D is wrong as the answers to the test amount to 'information' that cannot be stolen. Electricity (from charging the phone) also cannot be stolen.

■ KEY CASES, RULES, STATUTES AND INSTRUMENTS

The SQE1 Assessment Specification does not require you to know any case names for the topic of theft offences. It has identified, however, that candidates must know ss 1, 8, 9 and 10 of the Theft Act 1968.

8

Fraud offences

■ MAKE SURE YOU KNOW

This chapter will cover the core principles of criminal liability for the offence of fraud. Fraud is capable of being committed in three separate ways: fraud by false representation, fraud by abuse of position and fraud by failure to disclose information. You are required to know each offence in turn, and be able to apply these legal principles and rules appropriately and effectively to realistic client-based and ethical problems and situations for your SQE1 assessment.

The SQE1 Assessment Specification has not identified that candidates are required to recall/recite any case names, or statutory materials, for the topic of fraud.

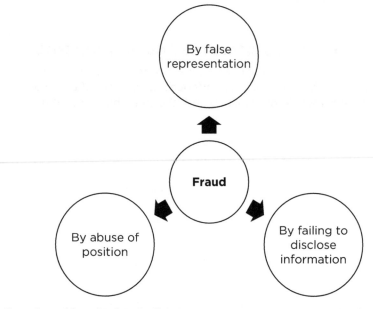

Overview of fraud-related offences

■ SQE ASSESSMENT ADVICE

As you work through this chapter, remember to pay particular attention in your revision to:

- the common elements shared between the offences, for example the requirements that the defendant must be 'dishonest' in his conduct and must intend, by his conduct, to make a gain or cause a loss for another
- the differences between each offence and how those differences will impact on the offence charged by the prosecution.

■ WHAT DO YOU KNOW ALREADY?

Have a go at these questions before reading this chapter. If you find some difficult or cannot remember the answers, make a note to look more closely at that area during your revision.

1) What is the meaning of 'fraud' in the Fraud Act (FA) 2006?

   [Introducing fraud, page 184]

2) True or false: there is a requirement that the defendant, as a result of his conduct, actually causes a gain or loss to another in order to be liable for fraud.

   [Fraud by false representation, pages 184–193]

3) Is dishonesty in fraud assessed subjectively or objectively?

   [Fraud by false representation, pages 184–193]

4) Fill in the blank: a person is guilty of fraud by failing to disclose information where they are under a _____.

   [Fraud by failing to disclose information, pages 193–196]

5) What do you understand the term 'occupy a position' to mean in the context of fraud by abuse of position?

   [Fraud by abuse of position, pages 196–198]

INTRODUCING FRAUD

The offence of fraud is contained in s 1 of the FA 2006.

For the purposes of the SQE1 assessment, you are required to understand the three ways in which fraud may be committed, namely:
• fraud by false representation
• fraud by failing to disclose information
• fraud by abuse of position.

'Fraud' is not defined in the statute and you must understand the various circumstances in which fraud may arise/may be proven in order to understand it. The remainder of this chapter will focus on each offence in turn.

FRAUD BY FALSE REPRESENTATION

The offence of fraud by false representation (FA 2006, s 2) can be broken down into five elements (see **Figure 8.1**). Each element is dealt with in turn below.

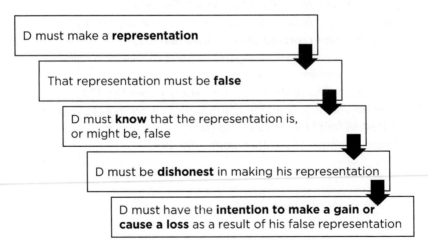

Figure 8.1: Elements of fraud by false representation

Representation

The first requirement is that the defendant makes a **representation**.

Key term: representation

A representation may concern a representation of fact, law or the state of mind of D or another.

Making a representation
If one is to 'make' a representation, they must simply communicate that representation. A representation may be express or implied. There is no limitation on the way in which a representation can then be made, which could be:
• orally
• in writing
• by conduct.

Exam warning

Please ensure that you do not misstate the law in this area. The only requirement is that a representation is *made*; it is not a requirement that the representation must be *received*. A multiple-choice question (MCQ) may suggest that the victim must see, hear or read the false representation; this is not relevant. Be clear as to what the requirement is: the representation must be *directed* at someone or something; it is not sufficient, for example, for a false representation to be made in a private diary that will not be conveyed to another.

Each of these are considered in **Table 8.1** (overleaf).

Additional points on representation
Some final questions on representation are dealt with in **Table 8.2**. Consider whether you know the answer to the question first, and then see the answer provided.

False representation
The second requirement is that the defendant makes a **false representation.**

Key term: false representation

A representation is false if it is untrue or misleading and the person making it knows that it is, or might be, untrue or misleading.

We shall first focus on the representation itself being false and then will consider the knowledge requirement (see **knowledge that the**

Table 8.1: Meaning of 'representation'

Type of representation	Explanation and examples
Fact	A representation as to fact refers to a communication as to present facts. For example: • Mark requests payment for some fence panels that had, in fact, already been paid for in full. The request for payment is an express representation that payment was expected. • Sam walks into an Oxford shop wearing a cap and gown and obtained goods on credit from the store. The wearing of the cap and gown was an implied representation that she was a fellow commoner of the university.
Law	A representation as to law refers to a communication as to the law of the land. For example, representations concerning matters of contract, tort or trusts law are caught by the FA 2006.
State of mind	A representation as to the state of mind of D, or another person, refers to the present intention of a person. For example, Sam orders a meal at a restaurant intending to pay. Sam later changes her mind but continued to dine at the restaurant. She had made a false representation as to her state of mind (ie the intention to pay).

representation is or might be false). From the outset, we can identify that 'false' bears two meanings within the FA 2006 (see **Table 8.3, page 188**):
• *untrue* representations
• *misleading* representations.

In any event, the representation *must* be untrue or misleading; it is not enough that the defendant merely believes that the representation be untrue or misleading.

Revision tip

Remember that D cannot be liable in circumstances where the representation is in fact true, even if D believed it to be false. The better offence will be attempted fraud (see **Chapter 3**). Likewise, if D makes a false representation but he mistakenly believes it is true, he cannot be liable for an offence of fraud.

Table 8.2: Additional questions on representation

Question	Answer
Does a representation have to be made to a human being?	No, a representation can be made to a machine. An example often given is where an individual enters a number into a 'chip and PIN' machine or bank details on an internet site. Importantly, it is irrelevant whether the machine requires any form of human input or involvement.
Does it matter if nobody believes the representation?	No, as fraud is a conduct crime, it is entirely irrelevant whether someone is tricked by the representation or not.
Can a representation be made by omission (ie a failure to act)?	Probably! While there is no direct case law on this topic, D could make a false representation where an individual makes a mistake as to a representation made by D, and D then fails to rectify or correct that mistake.
Given how wide the meaning of 'representation' is, is it possible to commit attempted fraud?	Yes, there are a number of limited circumstances in which an individual may be liable for attempted fraud. One example is where D prepares to make a false statement (eg by drafting false documentation) but is prevented from communicating that representation to another (eg because he is apprehended by the police) – he has not yet made a 'representation' but will have attempted to do so. A second example is where D makes a representation that they believe to be false, but that turns out to be true.

What is the situation if a defendant overcharges for services rendered, for example overcharging for building works? Will that amount to a *false representation*?

See **Practice example 8.1**.

Practice example 8.1

John is the manager of a central heating and plumbing firm. John charges two elderly sisters grossly excessive prices for work done on their flat. For example, John charges the sisters £3,000 to repair their boiler, work that would only cost around £800. John and his firm are known to the sisters from work previously done for their family. The sisters trust John and assume that any price to be paid is a fair one.

Do you think John would be liable for fraud?

These were the facts of *R v Silverman* (1988) 86 Cr App R 213 (a case concerning the old offence of obtaining property by deception). The issue in respect of fraud would be whether an excessive quotation could amount to a false representation. In the Court of Appeal, Watkins LJ explained that the criminal law may apply if one party takes dishonest advantage of the other by representing the work as a fair charge that he knew, but that the other did not know, is dishonestly excessive.

Table 8.3: Meaning of 'false representation'

Type of falsity	Explanation and examples
Untrue	The word 'untrue' ought to be given its ordinary meaning (ie a lie) and a jury should not normally be offered a further explanation or analysis of the word.
	While the statute is silent on this point, the representation need not be wholly untrue, in the sense that it is an outright lie. It is possible for a representation to contain partial truths (ie only parts of the representation need to be untrue).
	Generally, whether a representation is 'untrue' will be a factual determination for the jury. Where, however, the representation refers to a statement of law, it will be for the judge to determine (as a question of law) whether the statement is untrue (see *R v Whatcott* [2019] EWCA Crim 1889, in which the assessment of whether the representation was untrue depended on the interpretation of contractual provisions and their enforceability as a matter of law).
Misleading	Misleading means 'less than wholly true and capable of an interpretation to the detriment of the victim'. 'Misleading' is a broader term than 'untrue', focusing on the interpretation afforded to the representation. A representation is capable of being misleading even if it is factually true.

Knowledge that the representation is or might be false

The defendant must know that the representation is, or might be, untrue or misleading. There are four potential variations to this element of the offence:

a) The defendant knows that the representation *is untrue*.

b) The defendant knows that the representation *might be untrue*.

c) The defendant knows that the representation *is misleading*.

d) The defendant knows that the representation *might be misleading*.

The key statement of law regarding the mens rea requirement of knowledge for the purposes of fraud now comes from *R v Augunas* [2013] EWCA Crim 2046 (see **Practice example 8.2**).

Practice example 8.2

Darius is a Lithuanian national and obtains a number of bank cards from a woman, who informs him that he needs such cards in order to secure a job in the UK. The woman instructs Darius to go to a department store and purchase a laptop computer using one of the bank cards, telling him that she had put £1,200 on the card to cover the purchase. Darius attempts to purchase the computer but it turns out that the card is bogus. The police are called and Darius is arrested. In interview, Darius claims that he had no knowledge that the bank cards were false.

Do you think Darius would be liable for fraud?

These were the facts of *R v Augunas*. The Court of Appeal quashed Darius's conviction for fraud on account that the trial judge at first instance had directed the jury that Darius could be guilty of fraud if there was a 'reasonable suspicion on his part' that the card was fake. McCombe LJ considered this to be a misdirection and clarified that it is not enough that D ought to have appreciated, or suspected, that the representation was or might be untrue or misleading. D must *know* the representation was or might be untrue or misleading.

In addition to knowledge that the representation was or might be untrue or misleading, the offence was also widened to include 'wilful blindness', which refers to the circumstances where a defendant deliberately closes his eyes to the risk of a representation being false, or where a defendant deliberately refrains from asking questions or making enquiries.

Exam warning

Look closely at the wording of the MCQ. It is common for MCQ distractors to include options involving objective states of mind (eg D *'ought to have'* or *'should have'* known that the representation is, or might be, untrue). As should be apparent from the wording of the statute, whether D has the requisite knowledge for a fraud offence is a subjective test asking what *D* knew. Keep an eye out for subjective- and objective-style terminology.

Dishonesty

The next requirement is that the defendant must be 'dishonest' in the making of his false representation. The test for dishonesty is identical to that of theft and related offences considered in **Chapter 7**.

Importantly, however, the circumstances listed in s 2(1) of the Theft Act 1968 (circumstances where a defendant is not dishonest) do not apply to offences under the FA 2006, nor is there an equivalent provision. A defendant cannot argue, therefore, that they held an honest belief that they had a right in law to make a false representation (though if such an honest belief could be held, it may be relevant to the question of dishonesty under *Ivey v Genting Casinos (UK) Ltd t/a Crockfords* [2017] UKSC 67 – see **Chapter 7**).

Intention to make a gain or cause a loss

The final element of the offence is that the defendant must intend by making the representation:

a) to make a gain for himself or another, or

b) to cause loss to another or to expose another to a risk of loss.

There are a number of principles from this element of the offence that require independent consideration.

No actual loss required: intention-focused

The word 'intends' carries with it the ordinary meaning of intention discussed throughout this revision guide (ie direct intention or oblique intention). For example, a defendant may be liable for fraud in circumstances where it is virtually certain that the victim would suffer a loss as a result of the representation and the defendant appreciated that certainty.

Exam warning

Fraud by false representation is a conduct crime (see **Chapter 1**). This means that it is not necessary for the gain or loss to actually take place; the focus is on D's intention to make a gain or cause a loss. Ensure that you are aware of this when attempting an MCQ that focuses on this element.

Requirement of causation

The defendant must intend to make a gain or loss 'by making the representation'. This is a simple requirement for a causal link between the defendant's intention to make a gain/cause a loss and his false representation. Another way of explaining this is to ask if the defendant intended to make a gain or cause a loss *as a result* of his false representation (see **Practice example 8.3**).

Practice example 8.3

Stephanie wished to open a bank account. In attempting to open the account, Stephanie supplies the bank with false details as to her financial situation and savings in support of her application. At trial, the prosecution does not identify a particular gain or loss intended by Stephanie as a result of the representation at the bank but instead identified that she may gain future legitimate property developments as a result of the bank account being opened.

Do you think Stephanie would be liable for fraud?

These were the facts of *R v Gilbert* [2012] EWCA Crim 2392. The Court of Appeal quashed Stephanie's conviction for fraud on account that the trial judge at first instance had failed to direct the jury that there was a requirement for the gain or loss to be intended *as a result of* the representation.

Meaning of gain and loss

Importantly, there is no requirement for the defendant to intend to make a gain *and* cause a loss. This is evident in the wording of the statute, though, of course, the pair will often go hand in hand. 'Gain' and 'loss' are explained in s 5 FA 2006 and summarised in **Table 8.4**.

Table 8.4: Meaning of 'gain', 'loss' and other terms in s 5

Relevant terms	Explanation and examples
Gain	'Gain' includes keeping something you already have, as well as gaining something you do not already have.
Loss	'Loss' includes losing something that a person already has, or losing something they might get. Furthermore, D need not intend that the victim will actually suffer a loss – it is sufficient that D intends to expose the victim to a risk of loss (eg he may hope that the victim never actually suffers a loss, but he accepts that they may be at risk of such loss).
Permanent or temporary	The intention need not be for the gain or loss to be permanent; it can be an intention to gain or cause a loss on a temporary basis (eg D makes a false representation in order to borrow property from another).
Money or other property	The gain or loss must relate to money or other property. 'Property' is defined in a similar manner to that of theft in s 4 of the Theft Act 1968 (see **Chapter 7**). 'Property' does not extend to services (eg it is not fraud to intend to make a gain of a service).

Summary: what do we know about fraud by false representation?	
What is the meaning of 'representation'?	A representation is any form of communication, whether oral, in writing or by conduct. The representation can be expressly made or can be implied by the circumstances.
When is a representation 'false'?	A representation is false if it is untrue or is misleading. If the representation turns out to be true, the proper offence will be attempted fraud.
What does it mean that D must 'know' the representation is false?	D must know that the representation is, or might be, untrue or misleading. If D mistakenly believes that the representation is true, he cannot be liable for fraud.

What is the meaning of 'dishonesty'?	D must be objectively dishonest in the making of his representation. Whether D appreciated that he was dishonest is not relevant.
D must intend to make a 'gain or cause a loss to another'. What does this mean?	D must intend, as a result of his false representation, to make a gain for himself or another, or cause a loss to another/expose another to a risk of loss.

FRAUD BY FAILING TO DISCLOSE INFORMATION

The offence of fraud by failing to disclose information (FA 2006, s 3) can be broken down into four elements, as shown in **Figure 8.2**. All elements are dealt with in turn below.

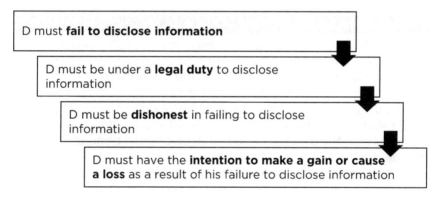

Figure 8.2: Elements of fraud by failing to disclose

Failure to disclose information

The first requirement is fairly straightforward, but does contain two fundamental principles (see **Table 8.5** overleaf).

Legal duty to disclose information

The second requirement is that the defendant must possess a **legal duty** to disclose the information.

Table 8.5: Meaning of failure to disclose information

Relevant terms	Explanation and examples
Failure to disclose	A 'failure' to disclose demonstrates that this offence criminalises omissions. The manner in which a failure to disclose may arise, however, varies. For example, a person may 'fail' to disclose in circumstances where he: • remains silent • says that there is nothing to disclose • discloses some information but withholds other information (ie he makes a partial disclosure).
Information	'Information' is an ordinary word and should be given its ordinary meaning. There is no requirement that the failure to disclose must relate to 'material' or 'relevant' information, nor is there any *de minimis* provision.

Key term: legal duty

No definition of 'legal duty' is provided in the FA 2006. In essence, a legal duty arises where there is a relationship between the parties that *imposes an obligation* on D to disclose information.

A legal duty may, for example, include a statutory duty, a contractual duty (whether in writing or not) and a fiduciary duty. A number of examples from the case law can be given here to demonstrate the scope of 'legal duty':
• When a defendant sought employment as a doctor, he had a duty to disclose that he had been suspended from practice.
• When a defendant applied for financial assistance, he had a duty to disclose other financial benefits he was in receipt of.

These facts should demonstrate that whether a legal duty exists is case-and-fact specific; the question of whether a legal duty exists is one of law for the judge, and not the jury. Importantly, the offence only concerns *legal* duties to disclose; a mere moral duty to disclose is insufficient.

Dishonesty and intention to make a gain/cause a loss
These final requirements are identical to that of fraud by false representation considered above. Some additional points can be made here:

- There is no requirement in law for the defendant to know that he is subject to a legal duty to disclose information. However, where the defendant is unaware of the existence of a legal duty, this may be relevant to determining whether he is dishonest to the standards of ordinary decent people.
- In terms of the intention to make a gain or cause a loss, there is no requirement that the intended loss is to be caused to a person to whom the legal duty is owed. Again, there is no requirement for the defendant to actually make a gain or cause a loss.
- There is a requirement, however, of a causal link between the defendant's intention to make a gain or cause a loss and his failure to disclose information.

Summary: what do we know about fraud by failing to disclose information?	
What is the meaning of 'failing to disclose information'?	A failure to disclose information will arise where D withholds information absolutely or partially.
When is there a 'legal duty' to disclose information?	A legal duty will arise where there is some form of relationship between D and another party imposing an obligation to disclose (eg a contract or fiduciary relationship).
What is the meaning of 'dishonesty'?	The requirement here is identical to that of fraud by false representation. In addition, while D need not be aware that he owes a legal duty, if he is unaware of the existence of a legal duty, this may affect the question of whether he is dishonest.
D must intend to make a 'gain or cause a loss to another'. What does this mean?	The requirement here is identical to that of fraud by false representation. In addition, it is not a requirement that the intended loss could be borne by the party to whom the legal duty was owed.

FRAUD BY ABUSE OF POSITION

The offence of fraud by abuse of position (FA 2006, s 4) can be broken down into five elements, as shown in **Figure 8.3**. We shall deal with each element in turn below.

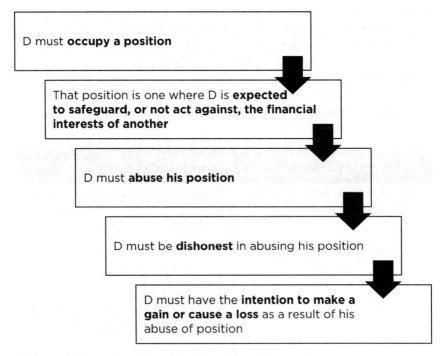

Figure 8.3: Elements of fraud by abuse of position

Occupation of a position

The first requirement is that the defendant 'occupies a position'. Neither the term 'occupies' nor 'position' are defined in the FA 2006. 'Occupies' is an ordinary word and requires no elaboration.

A 'position' is one that is of a fiduciary nature, or akin to a fiduciary relationship, see *Revise SQE Trusts Law* for guidance on the meaning of 'fiduciaries'. A fiduciary relationship involves one party (the 'fiduciary') who undertakes to act on behalf of another (the 'principal'), which gives rise to a relationship of trust and confidence. The distinguishing duty held by a fiduciary is often referred to as the undivided duty of loyalty. Below are some examples of fiduciary relationships:

• trustee and beneficiary

- director and company
- employee and employer.

Importantly, these are just examples and the courts have been clear that the notion of 'position' also extends to relationships that are *akin* to a fiduciary relationship. The question of whether the defendant occupied such a privileged position is one of law for the judge.

Expectation to safeguard
The position occupied by the defendant must be one for which there is an **expectation to safeguard**.

Key term: expectation to safeguard

D must possess an expectation to safeguard, which means he must:
- safeguard the financial interests of another person, or
- not act against the financial interests of another person.

The word 'expected' refers to the expectations of a reasonable member of the public, as personified by the jury.

Abuse of position
The third requirement is that there must be an **abuse of position**. The term 'abuse' is not, however, defined in the statute and is intended to cover a wide range of conduct.

Key term: abuse of position

Abuse of position means 'uses incorrectly' or 'puts to improper use' the position occupied, in a manner that is contrary to the expectation that arises because of that position.

The explanatory notes to the FA 2006 provide three helpful examples of defendants occupying positions and abusing them:
- 'An employee who fails to take up the chance of a crucial contract in order that an associate or rival company can take it up instead at the expense of the employer, commits an offence under this section.'
- 'An employee of a software company who uses his position to clone software products with the intention of selling the products on would commit an offence under this section.'
- 'A person who is employed to care for an elderly or disabled person [and] has access to that person's bank account and abuses his position by transferring funds to invest in a high-risk business venture of his own.'

Whether an occupied position has been abused is a question of fact for the jury. Importantly, while all of these examples concern positive acts on the part of the defendant, fraud by abuse of position can be committed by omission.

Dishonesty and intention to make a gain/cause a loss

These final requirements are identical to those considered above. Some additional points can be made here:

- D is not required to know that he occupies a position, though that may be relevant to the question of dishonesty.
- There is a requirement of a causal link between the defendant's intention to make a gain or cause a loss and his abuse of the position.

Summary: what do we know about fraud by abuse of position?	
When will D 'occupy a position'?	D will occupy a position relevant to the offence if he acts in a fiduciary capacity to another person, or in a relationship akin to that of a fiduciary.
What does it mean that D is 'expected to safeguard' the financial interests of another?	D is expected to safeguard, or not act against, the financial interests of another party. This 'expectation' is an objective test, asking what the reasonable man would expect in the circumstances.
What is the meaning of 'abuse' of position?	D abuses his position if he acts contrary to the expectation that he will safeguard another person's financial interests.
What is the meaning of 'dishonesty'?	The requirement here is identical to that of fraud by false representation and fraud by failing to disclose information. In addition, while D need not be aware that he occupies a position, if he is unaware, this may affect the question of whether he is dishonest.
D must intend to make a 'gain or cause a loss to another'. What does this mean?	The requirement here is identical to that of fraud by false representation and fraud by failing to disclose information. In addition, it is not a requirement that the intended loss could be borne by the party to whom the legal duty was owed.

■ KEY POINT CHECKLIST

This chapter has covered the following key knowledge points. You can use these to structure your revision, ensuring you recall the key details for each point, as covered in this chapter.

- Fraud is a single offence, which may be committed in three different ways.
- Fraud by false representation is committed where a defendant dishonestly makes a false representation, knowing that it is, or might be, untrue or misleading, with the intention to make a gain or cause a loss to another as a result of his false representation.
- Fraud by failing to disclose information is committed where a defendant dishonestly fails to disclose information in circumstances where he owes a legal duty to disclose information, and does so with an intention to make a gain or cause loss to another as a result of his failure to disclose information.
- Fraud by abuse of position is committed where a defendant dishonestly abuses an occupied position that he is expected to safeguard with the intention to make a gain or cause a loss to another as a result of his abuse of position.

■ KEY TERMS AND CONCEPTS

- representation (**page 185**)
- false representation (**page 185**)
- legal duty (**page 194**)
- expectation to safeguard (**page 197**)
- abuse of position (**page 197**)

■ SQE1-STYLE QUESTIONS

QUESTION 1

A woman orders a shirt from an online store, costing £30, and the shirt is delivered to her home. Several days later, the woman enters a physical store requesting a refund on the purchased shirt on account that it is unsuitable. In fact, the woman had taken a different shirt, from a different retailer, to the shop seeking a 'refund' for that shirt. The shop assistant is suspicious, does not grant the refund and contacts the police. The woman claims that she was unaware that she had brought a shirt from a different retailer but has no evidence to support this contention. The prosecution claim that the woman did know that the shirt was from a different retailer. The trial judge directs the jury that it is for them to decide whether they believe the woman's version of events or not. The jury accept the prosecution's case and convict the woman. The woman appeals to the Court of Appeal against her conviction.

Is the woman guilty of fraud?

A. Yes, the woman has dishonestly made a false representation in returning a shirt from a different retailer with the intention to make a gain of £30. Furthermore, the woman should have known that her representation was, or might be, untrue.

B. No, the trial judge was wrong to direct the jury that whether the woman knew that the representation was untrue was a question of fact for the jury to determine. Given that knowledge focuses on the state of mind of the woman, this is a question of law for the judge.

C. No, the woman did not have the necessary intention to make a gain or cause a loss on account that she was entitled to a refund if the shirt was unsuitable.

D. Yes, the woman has dishonestly made a false representation in returning a shirt from a different retailer with the intention to make a gain of £30. Whether the woman had sufficient knowledge that the representation was, or might be, untrue was a question of fact determined by the jury.

E. No, the refund was never given by the shop, therefore the woman cannot be guilty of fraud as she never actually made a gain or caused a loss.

QUESTION 2

A man seeks to sell his motorcycle in order to make some money. The man informs a potential buyer that the motorcycle is free from encumbrances and can be sold without restrictions. The man believes this representation to be false as he executed a document to mortgage the motorcycle to a finance company. If this were true, the motorcycle would not be free from encumbrances. The document, however, has not been validly executed and the motorcycle is, in fact, free from encumbrances. The man's representation is therefore true, despite his belief that it was false. The buyer is suspicious and has his doubts that the representation is true. The buyer does not purchase the motorcycle.

Is the man guilty of fraud?

A. No, while the man believed his representation to be false, it was in fact true. The offence of fraud requires the representation to be false in fact and the man cannot be guilty if the representation is true.

B. Yes, the invalidly executed document should not prevent the man from being guilty of fraud. The man intended to make a gain from selling the motorcycle and did so dishonestly; that is sufficient.

C. No, the buyer does not believe that the representation is true and therefore the man cannot be liable for fraud.

D. Yes, it is irrelevant whether the representation itself was false or not. The offence of fraud merely requires that the man believes that the representation is, or might be, false.

E. No, while the buyer need not be induced to purchase the motorcycle, he must believe that the representation is true. Given that the buyer did not believe that the representation made by the man was true, the man cannot be guilty of fraud.

QUESTION 3

A woman is a car dealer by trade. She is approached by a potential customer who is interested in purchasing a car. The customer identifies that he does not know anything about cars and is relying on the advice provided by the woman. The women sells a second-hand car for £10,000 when she knows that the car is only valued between £3,000 and £3,500.

Is the woman guilty of fraud by false representation?

A. No, the customer must take responsibility in these circumstances and should be aware of the trade practices adopted by salespersons.

B. Yes, the woman took advantage of the customer's lack of knowledge and abused her position as a salesperson when selling the car at a price above its value.

C. No, the representation made by the woman is not false. While the value of the car is significantly less than the price charged, the woman has the right to charge whatever amount she deems acceptable for the car. In such a case, there cannot be a false representation.

D. Yes, the customer has relied upon the skill and experience of the woman and trusts that the price to be paid will be a fair one. The woman has made a false representation that the price charged is fair and is reflective of the value of the car.

E. No, the woman is not dishonest in making the representation on account that she would not appreciate that such excess pricing was dishonest according to the standards of ordinary decent people.

QUESTION 4

A man works in a supermarket as a checkout operator. The man serves one of his friends and uses his staff discount card to reduce the bill owed by the customer. The supermarket's policy is clear that staff discount is only available to staff members, and is not available for use by family members or friends. The man is aware of this policy and chooses to ignore it because he does not think the policy is fair.

Is the man guilty of fraud by abuse of position?

A. Yes, the man has abused his position as an employee of the supermarket, for which the reasonable man would expect him to safeguard and not act against the financial interests of his employer. The man intends to make a gain for his friend, by paying for a reduced bill, and is dishonest in his conduct.

B. No, the man does not occupy a 'privileged' position as a checkout operator. The man is not of a sufficient seniority to owe a fiduciary duty to his employer and cannot be liable for fraud.

C. No, the man is not dishonest as he does not consider there is anything wrong with his conduct (thinking the policy is unfair) and is, therefore, unlikely to appreciate that he is dishonest according to the standards of ordinary and decent people.

D. No, it is doubtful that the man would consider that he is expected to safeguard the financial interests of his employer. If the man does not consider that he is expected to safeguard those interests, he cannot be liable for fraud.

E. Yes, the man has abused his position as an employee of the supermarket, for which the employer would expect him to safeguard and not act against the financial interests of his employer. The man intends to make a gain for his friend, by paying for a reduced bill, and is dishonest in his conduct.

QUESTION 5

A man creates a profile on a dating app and describes himself as a 'millionaire, with a wide portfolio of properties'. In reality, he is bankrupt, owns no property and lives with his parents. A woman responds to his profile and invites him round for dinner. They have sex and he later informs her that the information in his profile was false. She says she only had sex with him as she had believed the details were true and she would not have had sex with him had she have known they were false.

Is the man guilty of fraud by false representation?

A. Yes, he has made a false statement of fact that led to a gain, specifically sex.

B. Yes, even if the woman had not had sex with him, he had intended to make a gain from his false statement of fact.

C. No, the false statement must result in a gain for the man and a loss to the other party. While the man has gained, in the sense of sexual intercourse, there is no loss to the woman.

D. No, the woman was under an obligation to check whether the statement of fact was true before engaging in sexual intercourse with the man.

E. No, sexual intercourse does not amount to a gain for the purposes of fraud by false representation.

■ ANSWERS TO QUESTIONS

Answers to 'What do you know already?' questions at the start of the chapter

1) 'Fraud' is not defined in the FA 2006. Rather, the statute identifies that a single offence of fraud exists that is capable of being committed in three different circumstances.

2) False. Fraud is a conduct crime requiring proof that the defendant intended to cause himself or another to make a gain, or to cause a loss to another. There is no requirement that an individual actually makes a gain or suffers a loss.

3) Dishonesty is to be assessed objectively. First, the jury must ascertain the state of knowledge of the defendant and then, using

that knowledge, identify whether the defendant is dishonest by the standards of ordinary decent people.

4) A person is guilty of fraud by failing to disclose information where they are under a legal duty to disclose information and intend, by failing to disclose information, to make a gain or cause a loss.

5) The relevant occupied position for fraud by abuse of position is a fiduciary duty, or an obligation akin to a fiduciary duty.

Answers to end-of-chapter SQE1-style questions

Question 1:

The correct answer was D. This is because the woman must know (subjectively, not objectively, so option A is incorrect) that the representation was untrue, and this is a question of fact for the jury (so option B is incorrect). The jury has accepted the evidence from the prosecution. It is irrelevant that the refund was never given (so option E is incorrect). Option C cannot be correct on account that the woman was not entitled to a refund if she had not provided the correct piece of clothing for return.

Question 2:

The correct answer was A. This is because there is a requirement that the representation be in fact false. If the representation turns out to be true, there cannot be liability for fraud. An offence of attempted fraud may be charged in its place. All other options misstate the law.

Question 3:

The correct answer was D. This is because the excess price will be considered a false representation (specifically that the price charged is fair and reflective of the value of the car – so option C is incorrect). The woman will be objectively dishonest in doing so (it being irrelevant whether the woman appreciated that such was the case – so option E is incorrect). While the customer does have a responsibility to be aware of sale practices and techniques, this does not rid the woman of liability (so option A is incorrect). Option B is incorrect as it misstates the elements of the offence of fraud by false representation.

Question 4:

The correct answer was A. This is because the expectation to safeguard the interests of the employer is to be determined by what the reasonable man would expect of the defendant (thus options D and E are incorrect). The man certainly occupies a position as a fiduciary in his capacity as an employee (so option B is incorrect) and it is irrelevant whether the man appreciates that his conduct is dishonest (so option C is incorrect).

Question 5:

The correct answer was E. This is because sexual intercourse does not amount to 'money or other property' for the purposes of the FA 2006. All other options are therefore incorrect.

■ KEY CASES, RULES, STATUTES AND INSTRUMENTS

The SQE1 Assessment Specification does not require you to know any case names, or statutory materials, for the topic of fraud. Despite this, you are strongly advised to read ss 1–5 of the FA 2006, including the relevant explanatory notes, in full and the associated case law interpreting that statute.

9

Criminal damage

■ MAKE SURE YOU KNOW

This chapter will cover the core principles of criminal liability for the offences of simple criminal damage, aggravated criminal damage and arson. You are required to know each offence in turn, and be able to apply these legal principles and rules appropriately and effectively to realistic client-based and ethical problems and situations for your SQE1 assessment.

The SQE1 Assessment Specification has not identified that candidates are required to recall/recite any case names, or statutory materials, for the topic of criminal damage.

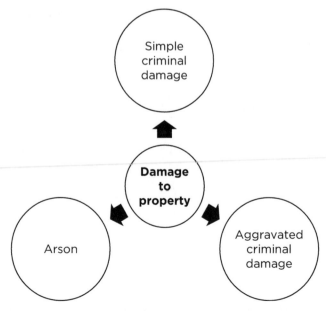

Overview of criminal damage offences

■ SQE ASSESSMENT ADVICE

As you work through this chapter, remember to pay particular attention in your revision to:

- the definition, or lack thereof, of 'damage'
- the distinction between simple and aggravated criminal damage and arson
- the subtle differences in actus reus and mens rea between simple and aggravated criminal damage
- the defence of lawful excuse.

■ WHAT DO YOU KNOW ALREADY?

Have a go at these questions before reading this chapter. If you find some difficult or cannot remember the answers, make a note to look more closely at that area during your revision.

1) How do the courts understand 'damage' for the purposes of criminal damage?

   [Simple criminal damage, pages 208–218]

2) True or false: in order to be liable for aggravated criminal damage, the defendant must have endangered the life of another.

   [Aggravated criminal damage, pages 218–221]

3) Fill in the blank: the offence of arson requires damage or destruction to be caused by _____.

   [Arson, pages 221–223]

INTRODUCTION TO CRIMINAL DAMAGE

Criminal damage is an offence against **property**. For the purposes of the SQE1 assessment, you are required to understand:

* simple criminal damage
* aggravated criminal damage
* arson.

All three offences are provided for in s 1 of the Criminal Damage Act (CDA) 1971. The remainder of this chapter will consider each offence in turn.

SIMPLE CRIMINAL DAMAGE

The offence of simple criminal damage can be broken down into five elements, as detailed in **Figure 9.1**.

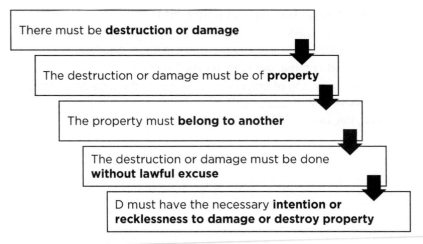

Figure 9.1: Elements of simple criminal damage

Destruction or damage

The first requirement for the offence of simple criminal damage is that there must have been damage or destruction of property. Neither term is defined in the legislation; the court adopts a common-sense understanding and whether there has been destruction or damage is to be determined on a case-by-case basis (see **Practice example 9.1**).

Practice example 9.1

Paul was being held in a police cell and while he was in the cell, he smeared mud on the walls as graffiti. No permanent damage was caused; the walls were cleaned and returned to the condition they had been in previously. The cleaning cost £7.

Do you think this would be classed as criminal damage?

These were the facts of *Roe v Kingerlee* [1986] Crim LR 735. Woolf LJ in the Divisional Court ruled that what constitutes criminal damage is a 'matter of fact and degree' applying common sense. Paul had caused damage in this case.

Given the inclusion of 'or' in the statute, it is to be understood that destruction and damage are not synonyms; they involve two separate circumstances. If one destroys property, they will inevitably damage it; however, property that is damaged is not necessarily destroyed.

'Destroy'

The term **destroy** (and 'destruction') are non-contentious and are generally self-explanatory.

Key term: destroy

To 'destroy' means 'to render useless', so destruction involves an element of finality and totality about it.

The following would amount to a destruction within the meaning of the CDA 1971:
• demolishing a building
• burning books
• killing a pet.

'Damage'

'**Damage**' has proved more contentious. Given the lack of statutory definition, the courts have had to address the meaning of damage.

Key term: damage

A traditional understanding of 'damage' can be said to involve some form of 'physical damage' (eg a scratch to a car, a cracked window). However, the courts seem to understand damage to mean rendering something 'imperfect' or 'inoperative'. This may be so due to the value of the property being reduced, or the time and effort involved in returning the property to its previous state.

Table 9.1 identifies some of the themes adopted by the courts in determining whether property has been damaged.

Table 9.1: Meaning of 'damage'

Theme	Explanation and examples
Impairment of value or usefulness	If there has been a permanent or temporary impairment of value or usefulness of the property, this may amount to criminal damage. For example: • *R v Fiak* [2005] EWCA Crim 2381: flooding a prison cell by stuffing a blanket into a toilet and flushing repeatedly was held to amount to damage given that the blanket, the cell and the adjoining cells could not be used until they were cleaned and dried out. • *Drake v DPP* [1994] Crim LR 855: the application of stickers to a car windscreen and the clamping of a car could not be said to impair the integrity of that car.
Time, effort and expense to rectify damage	If the property is capable of being restored to its condition prior to the conduct of D, a court may find that damage exists if restoration of the property requires time, effort or expense. All factors (ie time and effort) are not required; each case will be determined on its own facts. For example: • *Hardman v Chief Constable of Avon and Somerset* [1986] Crim LR 330: a water-based paint that had been applied to pavements as part of a protest was considered damage due to the time and expense in removing it. It was irrelevant that the paint would have washed away in the rain (NB this was a Crown Court case). • *A (a juvenile) v R* [1978] Crim LR 689: spitting on a police officer's coat did not amount to damage, with the Crown Court finding that there was no effort or expense in removing the spittle, nor did the spittle render the coat imperfect.

The type of property may also be relevant in determining whether there is damage (eg a scratch on a scaffold pole may not be considered damage, as such scratches are a common occurrence, whereas a scratch on a car bonnet will be considered damage).

Additional points on damage and destruction

Some final questions on destruction and damage are dealt with in **Table 9.2**. Consider whether you know the answer to the question first, and then see the answer provided.

Table 9.2: Additional questions on damage and destruction

Question	Answer
Does damage or destruction need to be permanent?	The term 'destroy' would involve a permanent outcome in respect of the property. 'Damage', on the other hand, does not require such permanence; criminal damage may be committed even if the damage is only temporary.
Can destruction or damage arise as a result of an omission, or must it involve a positive act?	The CDA 1971 is silent as to whether the words 'destroy or damage' require a positive act, or may be committed by omission. Following *R v Miller* [1983] 2 AC 61 (considered in **Chapter 1**), however, it is evident that destruction and damage can be committed by way of omission, so long as a duty to act can be identified (eg a duty to rectify a dangerous situation).
Can computer programs be damaged or destroyed?	The modification of the contents of a computer does not amount to damage unless the effect of that modification is that it 'impairs its physical condition'. This does not mean that the damage has to be tangible; the addition or deletion of files from a computer disk can amount to 'damage'.

Property

The second element of the offence of simple criminal damage is that what is damaged or destroyed amounts to **property**.

Key term: property

The meaning of 'property' is provided in s 10(1) CDA 1971. In summary, 'property' means property of a tangible nature, whether real or personal, including money.

We considered the meaning of 'property' in **Chapter 7** (which you should reconsider). **Table 9.3** provides an overview of property for the purposes of criminal damage.

Table 9.3: Meaning of 'property'

Explanation of 'property' in s 10(1) CDA 1971	Is it property?
'Tangible' property is an umbrella term for property that can be seen and touched. Intangible property (such as copyright, for example) cannot be damaged within the meaning of the CDA 1971.	YES
'Real' property simply means land (also known as 'realty'). Land can be damaged, for example, by dumping chemicals on it or digging it up.	
'Personal' property means anything other than land, such as a watch.	
Wild creatures are capable of amounting to 'property' so long as they are tamed/ordinarily kept in captivity (eg a lion in a zoo). A wild creature can also amount to 'property' if it has been 'reduced into possession' (eg by catching a wild creature in a trap). Naturally, a household pet will amount to 'property' and can be damaged or destroyed.	YES
Wild plants and fungi do not amount to 'property' for the purposes of the CDA 1971. Plants and fungi that are not wild (ie they are owned by someone) will amount to property and are capable of being damaged or destroyed.	NO

Exam warning

You will notice that there are subtle differences between theft and criminal damage in respect of property. It is important not to confuse the two and to ensure that you are satisfied with the rules as they apply specifically to criminal damage. For example, land cannot generally be stolen, but it can be damaged/destroyed. Look out for this in SQE1.

Belonging to another

The property, which has been damaged or destroyed, must 'belong to another'. We have come across the concept of belonging to another in **Chapter 7** in the context of theft; the principles for criminal damage are very similar.

The property in question must belong to *another* person (see **Table 9.4**). This means that a defendant cannot be liable for simple criminal damage if he damages or destroys his own property that is not subject to any right or interest by another party. This is a distinguishing feature between simple and aggravated criminal damage.

Table 9.4: Meaning of 'belonging to another'

When property will belong to another	Explanation
If another has custody or control	If an individual has possession of property they are said to have 'custody or control' of it. In that regard, D is capable of damaging property (even his own), if another person has the custody or control over it. For example, Mark allows Sam to borrow his vacuum cleaner. As a practical joke, Mark removes the fuse from the vacuum plug. While Mark may lack the mens rea (see below), he has technically damaged property belonging to another as Sam has custody over the vacuum cleaner.
If another has a proprietary right or interest	This simply means that an individual has some sort of right over the property. For example, where property is owned by multiple individuals (as joint tenants, for example), then it is possible for one individual to damage the property belonging to the other tenants.
If another has a charge on it	A charge is simply a form of security over a piece of property. The most accessible example is a mortgage. If D sets fire to his house, which is subject to a mortgage, he can still be charged with criminal damage (and arson) as the mortgagee will have a proprietary right, namely a charge, over the property.
If the property is subject to a trust	This provision simply reflects the fact that property which is subject to a trust can be damaged or destroyed by the trustee (as the legal owner), given that the property also belongs to the beneficiary of a trust (as the beneficial owner). The rule applies equally vice versa.
If it is the property of a corporation	A corporation is recognised in law as having its own legal personality (separate from its shareholders and directors). As such, an incorporated body is capable of owning property; damage to that property will be considered as amounting to another even if done by a director or shareholder.

Without lawful excuse

The defendant must also act 'without lawful excuse'. In essence, this is a statutory defence to simple criminal damage, and is defined further in s 5 CDA 1971. Lawful excuse only applies to an offence of simple criminal damage (and simple arson). It does not, therefore, apply to aggravated criminal damage (or aggravated arson). An overview of lawful excuse is provided in **Table 9.5**.

Table 9.5: Meaning of 'without lawful excuse'

Lawful excuses in s 5(2)
The first lawful excuse arises where D believes that he has, or would have, consent to damage or destroy property. This is so even where a mistake, or several mistakes, have been made by D.
The second lawful excuse involves two conditions: a) The act of damage or destruction must have been done in order to protect property belonging to himself or another, and b) D believed that the property was in 'immediate need of protection' and believed that the means of protection adopted were 'reasonable in all the circumstances'.

Lawful excuse is a particularly complex defence, and it is worth breaking it down further.

Honest belief in consent

The first defence is that the defendant holds an honest belief in consent. This is a subjective test and involves a number of variations, which are identified in **Table 9.6**.

Table 9.6: Variations of an honest belief in consent

Variation in consent	Variation in provider of consent
1. D believes that he *has* been provided with consent to damage or destroy property.	1. The person who provides, or would provide, consent *is entitled* to do so.
2. D believes that he *would have* been provided with consent to damage or destroy property had the party providing consent known of the circumstances.	2. The person who provides, or would provide, consent *is believed to be entitled* to do so.

From this, you should be able to see that a defendant's belief may be mistaken, and this will not affect the operation of the defence. It is immaterial whether a belief is justified or not, so long as it is honestly held. Therefore, any mistake need not be a reasonable one, it need only be honest. For an example of this, see **Practice example 9.2**.

Practice example 9.2

Beverley is currently residing with her friend, Ronald. One evening, Beverley, intoxicated following a night on the town, returns home to find the door locked. Believing that Ronald would be okay with her actions, she breaks a window in an attempt to get into the property. Beverley's belief is mistaken, however, as, unfortunately, she has broken into the wrong house, which actually belongs to Patricia.

Would Beverley have a defence of lawful excuse here for the damage caused to the window?

These are the facts of *Jaggard v Dickinson* [1981] QB 527. The Divisional Court found that Beverley could rely on her honest, though mistaken, belief that consent would have been provided for the damage of property. It did not matter that the belief was induced by intoxication.

Jaggard v Dickinson illustrates a number of important points:
• A mistaken, though honest, belief in consent is sufficient to find a lawful excuse.
• Self-induced intoxication will not prevent an honest belief in consent from being relied upon.

The decision in *Jaggard* appears to be limited to cases of lawful excuse in criminal damage and should not be extended beyond this (see the effect of intoxication on other mistakes in **Chapter 4**).

Other property in need of protection
As noted in **Table 9.6**, this defence requires consideration of two conditions. **Table 9.7** deals with these two conditions in further detail.

Exam warning

Lawful excuse applies only to the defence of *property* in the immediate need of protection; it does not apply to the protection of *persons* in immediate need of protection. Be aware of this distinction for SQE1.

Table 9.7: Lawful excuse to protect property

Requirement	Explanation and examples
'in order to protect property'	This is an objective test. It asks whether D acted in order to protect property belonging to himself or another.
Belief that the property was in 'immediate need of protection' and the means adopted were 'reasonable'.	This is largely a subjective test based upon D's beliefs. First, D must believe that the property was in immediate need of protection. This then leads, however, to an objective question as to whether the property was actually in need of immediate protection.
	Second, D must believe that the means adopted were reasonable in the circumstances. Importantly, the means adopted need not *actually* be reasonable; the focus is on whether D *believed* those means to be reasonable in all the circumstances. So long as the belief is honestly held, it need not be reasonable.

Other lawful excuses

General defences are capable of providing a defendant with a 'lawful excuse' beyond that listed in the CDA 1971.

Intention or recklessness

The final element of the offence of simple criminal damage is that the defendant must either:

- intend to damage or destroy property belonging to another, or
- be reckless as to whether such property, belonging to another, would be damaged or destroyed.

Exam warning

The intention or recklessness must relate to the damage or destruction of property; an intention to harm another person cannot be transferred to an intention to cause damage (see **Chapter 1**).

Intention and recklessness were discussed in full in **Chapter 1**.

Exam warning

It is irrelevant that D does not believe what he does amounts to 'damage or destruction'; the focus is on whether D intended to do the act that amounts to damage. Make sure that you are aware of this principle and avoid being drawn into an answer that refers to D's belief being relevant.

Knowledge or belief that property belongs to another

The defendant must intend to destroy or damage property *belonging to another*. This demonstrates a requirement of knowledge or belief on the part of the defendant that the property belongs to another (see **Practice example 9.3**).

Practice example 9.3

David, a tenant of a flat, installed wiring beneath the floorboards. Unbeknown to him, and as a matter of property law, the installed wiring became part of the landlord's property (it became a fixture). When David came to leave the property, he caused £130 worth of damage by removing the wiring.

Is David liable for criminal damage?

These were the facts of *R v Smith* [1974] QB 354. The Court of Appeal found that David could not be liable for criminal damage in cases where he neither knew, nor believed, that the property belonged to another. David held an honest, though mistaken, belief that the property belonged to him.

Exam warning

This belief that property did not belong to another need *not* be reasonable nor justified. It is sufficient if the belief is honestly, but unreasonably, held.

Summary: what do we know about simple criminal damage?

What is the meaning of 'destroy' and 'damage'?	To 'destroy' property is to render it useless; destruction involves an element of finality. To 'damage' property is to render it imperfect or inoperative by impairing its value, usefulness or requiring time, effort or expense to be exercised to rectify the damage.

What is the meaning of 'property'?	Property refers to any tangible property, whether realty or personalty.
What is the meaning of 'belonging to another'?	To 'belong to another' means that some person other than D has some form of custody, control or proprietary right/interest in the property.
What is the meaning of 'without lawful excuse'?	Here, D either has a belief in consent or a belief that property is in need of protection.
What is the mens rea for criminal damage?	D must either intend to damage or destroy property, or be reckless to the thought of such property being damaged or destroyed. D must know or believe that the property belongs to another.

AGGRAVATED CRIMINAL DAMAGE

The offence of aggravated criminal damage can be broken down into five elements, considered in **Figure 9.2**.

Figure 9.2: Elements of aggravated criminal damage

The offence of aggravated criminal damage is largely identical to that of simple criminal damage. There are, however, some subtle differences that you must understand:

- Property need not belong to another; the offence can be committed where the defendant damages or destroys his *own* property.
- The statutory defence of lawful excuse does not apply to aggravated criminal damage.

See **Figure 9.3**.

Figure 9.3: Understanding the requirement of endangerment

Exam warning

Remember that aggravated criminal damage does not require the property to belong to another; it is sufficient for D to destroy or damage his own property with the intention of, or being reckless to, endangering the life of another. This is a common mistake that is made and often leads to candidates reaching the wrong conclusion.

Intention or recklessness to endanger life

The defendant must intend or be reckless as to **endangering life**.

Key term: endangering life

Endangerment to life focuses on the state of mind of D; there does not have to be any *actual* endangerment to life. Furthermore, D must intend or be reckless as to endangering the life *of another*. If D only intends (or is reckless) as to endangering his own life, no offence is committed.

The defendant must intend (or be reckless) as to the endangerment to life *by that destruction or damage*. This element is complex and can be understood in two separate notions:

a) The endangerment to life must have been caused by the damage itself, and not as a result of the act that caused the damage. Suppose

Mark shoots a rifle at a window, behind which Sam is stood. Mark is reckless as to the fact that the rifle shot would endanger Sam's life, but is not reckless as to the fact that Sam was endangered *by the destruction or damage of property* (ie the broken glass). In this case, Mark cannot be liable for aggravated criminal damage.

b) The words 'destruction or damage' in connection to endangerment of life are concerned with the *intended or reckless* destruction or damage that endangers life, not to the destruction or damage *actually caused.* For example, a defendant's actions may pose a serious risk to life, but the damage itself may only involve a trivial endangerment to life.

For a practical application of these principles, see **Practice example 9.4**.

Practice example 9.4

Luke has been involved in a dispute with his neighbours. One evening, he throws a brick through their window. He then threw a cannister of petrol through the hole in the window and a piece of paper that he had set light to. The paper failed to ignite the petrol and was swiftly extinguished. Luke has been charged with the offence of aggravated criminal damage on the basis that he had intentionally caused damage to the window and had been reckless as to whether the life of the occupants would be endangered.

Does this amount to the offence?

These are the facts of *R v Wenton* [2010] EWCA Crim 2361, who successfully appealed against his conviction. The Court of Appeal held that there were two distinct acts here (a) the breaking of the window (the act that caused the damage) and (b) putting the canister into the house (the act that endangered life). The criminal damage had not endangered life.

Revision tip

Aggravated criminal damage, whether charged intentionally or recklessly, is a specific-intent offence given the presence of an ulterior mens rea (ie endangering life – see **Chapter 4**). As you will appreciate, voluntary intoxication is, therefore, capable of acting as a defence to a charge of aggravated criminal damage to the extent that the prosecution must prove that the defendant formed the mens rea for the offence despite his intoxicated state.

Summary: what do we know about aggravated criminal damage?

The elements of aggravated criminal damage are very similar to that of simple criminal damage. There are, however, some differences between the two:

- The property damaged or destroyed need not belong to another.
- The defence of lawful excuse cannot be used for aggravated criminal damage.
- D must not only intend or be reckless as to the damage or destruction of property, but must intend or be reckless as to endangering the life of another as a result of the damage or destruction.

ARSON

Our final offence is that of **arson**.

Key term: arson

Arson is a separate offence to simple and aggravated criminal damage and is charged in circumstances where the destruction or damage is caused by fire.

The elements of arson depend on whether the circumstances are based upon simple or aggravated criminal damage (referred to as 'simple arson' and 'aggravated arson' – see **Table 9.8**).

Table 9.8: Elements of arson

Simple arson	Aggravated arson
a) There must be destruction or damage *by fire*.	a) There must be destruction or damage *by fire*.
b) The destruction or damage must be *of property*.	b) The destruction or damage must be *of property*.
c) The property must *belong to another*.	c) The destruction or damage must be done *without lawful excuse*.
d) The destruction or damage must be done *without lawful excuse*.	d) D must have the necessary *intention or recklessness* to damage or destroy property *by fire*.
e) D must have the necessary *intention or recklessness* to damage or destroy property *by fire*.	e) D must have the necessary *intention or recklessness* as to *endangering life by fire*.

Arson involves two subtle changes to both simple and aggravated criminal damage, which can be expressed as follows:

a) The property was destroyed or damaged *by fire.*

b) The defendant must intend or be reckless to the thought that property would be destroyed or damaged *by fire.*

As with aggravated criminal damage, should arson be charged as involving an endangerment to life, there is no requirement that the property belongs to another, nor is there a statutory defence of lawful excuse available.

Destruction or damage by fire

Any form of damage or destruction by fire is sufficient, whether this be a raging inferno or a simple flame. As with the understanding of 'damage' above, very slight physical damage caused by fire will be sufficient for arson. Damage caused by smoke from fire is not arson, however.

Intention or recklessness as to fire

The defendant must intend or be reckless that the damage or destruction be caused by fire. Where a defendant intends to damage property by a different means, but a fire unexpectedly breaks out and causes the damage, the defendant cannot be liable for intended arson (though you would question whether he was reckless).

Given that arson is a separate offence from simple and aggravated criminal damage, it is vital that a charge or indictment accurately charges a defendant with the offence of arson (see **Practice example 9.5**).

Practice example 9.5

Alan is alleged to have caused damage by fire to a window frame, door glass and pipes to the value of £1,141. The indictment makes no reference to the word 'arson' and simply reads that Alan damaged the said property 'by fire'.

Do you think this indictment has been properly drafted?

These were the facts of *R v Drayton* [2005] EWCA Crim 2013. Hedley J explained that to charge Alan with 'damage by fire' is sufficient as that is an accurate description of what arson is. His Lordship did go on to identify that 'while the use of the word "arson" is not mandatory, it might be helpful were it to be employed'.

Summary: what do we know about arson?
• Arson requires the damage or destruction to property to be caused by fire.
• D must intend or be reckless that such damage or destruction is caused by fire.
• It is desirable that D is charged with 'arson', but 'damage by fire' is acceptable.

■ KEY POINT CHECKLIST

This chapter has covered the following key knowledge points. You can use these to structure your revision, ensuring you recall the key details for each point, as covered in this chapter.

• Simple criminal damage is the damage or destruction of property belonging to another, without lawful excuse, and with the intention or recklessness that such property belonging to another will be destroyed or damaged.

• Aggravated criminal damage also requires the defendant intends or is reckless as to the endangerment of life as a result of the damage or destruction.

• Arson is a distinct offence involving damage caused by fire.

■ KEY TERMS AND CONCEPTS

• destroy (**page 209**)
• damage (**page 209**)
• property (**page 211**)
• endangering life (**page 219**)
• arson (**page 221**)

■ SQE1-STYLE QUESTIONS

QUESTION 1

A woman was heavily intoxicated having drunk significant quantities of alcohol while at a friend's house. The woman began taking glassware and throwing it against the wall, smashing it in the process. The woman's friend had expressed her dislike for the glassware earlier in the evening but did not consent to the woman damaging the property. The woman believed that her friend wanted her to damage the property.

Is the woman guilty of criminal damage?

A. Yes, while the woman held an honest but mistaken belief in consent of the owner of the property, the belief was not reasonable.

B. No, the woman held an honest but mistaken belief in consent of the owner, and it is irrelevant that she was intoxicated.

C. Yes, while the woman held an honest but mistaken belief in consent of the owner of the property, she cannot rely on lawful excuse if she is intoxicated.

D. Yes, consent was not provided for the damage to property and the woman cannot rely on a mistaken belief in consent.

E. No, the woman held a reasonable belief in consent of the owner.

QUESTION 2

A man believes that his daughter has been kidnapped and she is being held in a house. The man enters the house by breaking in the door. The man mistakenly believes that his daughter is in need of immediate protection and that damage to the property is justified. The daughter has not been kidnapped and was not in any immediate danger.

Is the man guilty of criminal damage?

A. No, while the man was acting in the belief that his daughter was in immediate need of protection, the means he adopted were not reasonable in the circumstances.

B. Yes, the man cannot rely on the fact that he damaged property in order to protect another person who was in immediate danger.

C. No, the man can rely on the fact that he damaged property in order to protect another person who was in immediate danger.

D. Yes, the daughter was never in any immediate danger; a mistaken belief as to immediate danger is not sufficient.

E. No, the man believed that his daughter was in danger; a mere belief, albeit mistaken, is sufficient.

QUESTION 3

A man breaks into an office block one night, intending to steal. On leaving the premises, the man sets fire to the offices. There were two flats above the offices. No occupants were home at the time the fire broke out. The man did not know that there were flats above the offices.

The man did not consider any person was in the building at the time. The man is charged with aggravated arson.

Is the man guilty of aggravated arson?

A. Yes, the man should have foreseen that the endangerment to life was a virtually certain consequence of his actions.

B. No, the man cannot be guilty of aggravated arson because no lives were actually endangered.

C. Yes, while the man did not intend that life be endangered, he should have foreseen a risk that life could be endangered as a result of the damage.

D. No, the man did not intend, nor did he foresee a risk, that life would be endangered as a result of the damage.

E. Yes, the man intended to cause damage by fire and that is sufficient for the offence of arson.

QUESTION 4

A teenage boy, aged 14, threw stones at an elderly neighbour who had shouted at him for playing games near his garden. One of the stones missed the neighbour and broke the window. The boy intentionally threw the stones at the neighbour but did not intend to cause any damage to the window. The boy did not foresee a risk that the window would be damaged.

Is the boy guilty of criminal damage?

A. No, the boy must intend to cause damage, or be reckless as to causing damage. A mere intention to do the act that causes the damage is not enough.

B. Yes, the boy has thrown the stone intentionally. By throwing the stone intentionally, the boy must accept any damage that arises as a result.

C. Yes, the boy's intention to throw the stone at the neighbour can be transferred to the damaged window.

D. No, the boy has a lawful excuse for throwing the stones given that the neighbour had shouted at him.

E. Yes, while the boy did not foresee the risk of damage to the window, another boy of his age would have foreseen the risk of such damage occurring.

QUESTION 5

After a dispute at work, a scientist who had been researching genetic sequencing destroyed the squirrels he had been using in his research. He had destroyed them intending to set back his employers' research by months. The man had been in sole charge of the welfare of the squirrels and claimed they were his to do with as he pleased.

Is the man guilty of criminal damage?

A. No, the squirrels cannot be construed as property as they are wild creatures.

B. No, the squirrels had been reduced into possession and amounted to property, but they belonged to the man who had custody and control of the squirrels.

C. Yes, the squirrels had been reduced into possession and therefore amounted to property. The squirrels were also property that belonged to the employer.

D. No, animals do not amount to property for the offence of criminal damage and cannot then belong to another.

E. Yes, all animals are property for the offence of criminal damage.

■ ANSWERS TO QUESTIONS

Answers to 'What do you know already?' questions at the start of the chapter

1) Damage is not defined in the statute; the common law has adopted a number of principles to determine whether 'damage' exists. For example, damage may be found where the property has been rendered imperfect or inoperative and where time, effort and expense are required to rectify the damage. Damage must be considered on a case-by-case basis as a matter of fact and degree.

2) False. Aggravated criminal damage is an ulterior-intent offence. While the defendant must intend or be reckless as to the thought of endangering life, there is no requirement that life be actually endangered.

3) The offence of arson requires damage or destruction to be caused by fire. A defendant will be charged with aggravated arson where the fire endangers life.

Answers to end-of-chapter SQE1-style questions

Question 1:

The correct answer was B. This is because the woman may rely on an honest, albeit mistaken, belief in consent, even if induced by intoxication. Options A and E are incorrect as the belief need not be reasonable. Option C is incorrect as a mistake induced by intoxication appears to be acceptable for criminal damage. Option D is incorrect as it ignores the fact that the defence of lawful excuse is concerned with the woman's belief in consent.

Question 2:

The correct answer was B. This is because the protection of another person is not a lawful excuse. All other answers appear to identify that protection of another person is sufficient to found a lawful excuse.

Question 3:

The correct answer was D. Given that the man did not know that there were flats above the office block, nor did he think anyone was in the building, he cannot have intended such endangerment, nor could he have been subjectively reckless. Option A is incorrect because virtual certainty is a subjective test, not an objective one. Option B is wrong because it is irrelevant whether lives were actually endangered; the focus is whether the man intended or was reckless as to endangerment. Option C is incorrect because recklessness is a subjective test, not an objective one. Option E is incorrect because it omits the second mens rea requirement that the man must intend or be reckless as to the thought of life being endangered.

Question 4:

The correct answer was A. This is because a mere intention to do the act causing damage is insufficient (so option B is wrong); the boy must intend to cause damage or destruction as a result of that act, or be reckless. The boy's intention cannot be transferred from a person to property, so option C is incorrect. Option D is wrong as no such lawful excuse exists. Option E is wrong as it misstates the mens rea element of the offence.

Question 5:

The correct answer was C. This is because wild animals can amount to property but only if tamed, ordinarily kept in captivity or where they have been reduced into possession (therefore options A and D are incorrect). The property belongs to another if another party has custody and control over it and even though the man may assert the squirrels were in his custody, another party (the employer) certainly has a right over that property (so option B is wrong). Option E is wrong as only animals that are tamed are classed as property.

■ KEY CASES, RULES, STATUTES AND INSTRUMENTS

The SQE1 Assessment Specification does not require you to know any case names, or statutory materials, for the topic of criminal damage. Despite this, you are strongly advised to read ss 1, 5 and 10 of the CDA 1971 in full and the associated case law interpreting that statute.

Index